The Bunnysitters

By Kate Banks

Illustrated by Blanche Sims

A STEPPING STONE BOOK

Random House New York

For Camila and Lucas

—K. B.

Library of Congress Cataloging-in-Publication Data
Banks, Kate, 1960–
    The bunnysitters / by Katherine Banks ; illustrations by Blanche
Sims.
        p. cm.
    "A Stepping Stone book."
    Summary: Hoping to make enough money so they can finish building a
derby car, two boys offer to take care of a neighbor's rabbit.
    ISBN 0-679-81232-6 (pbk.)—ISBN 0-679-91232-0 (lib. bdg.)
    [1. Rabbits—Fiction. 2. Pets—Fiction.] I. Sims, Blanche, ill.
II. Title.
PZ7.B22594Bu 1991
[E]—dc20   90-27441

Manufactured in the United States of America 1 2 3 4 5 6 7 8 9 0

CONTENTS

1. Money Doesn't Grow on Trees

Nicholas Buchanan was about to turn ten. Turning ten meant you could have your own library card and your own locker at school. It meant you could get into the movies without your parents. But the best thing about turning ten was the Archie B. Ball Annual Soapbox Derby. You had to be ten to enter. And you had to be able to build a race car practically all by yourself.

Nicholas clutched an imaginary steering wheel and drove his foot into the ground. "We're coming up on the finish," he cried. "That's it, folks! Buchanan wins by a hair."

"Fat chance!" laughed his best friend, Alex. "But as they say, may the best man win."

"That's right," said Nicholas. "And may his best friend come in second."

* * *

Nicholas and Alex had been looking forward to the derby all year. Now it was just eight weeks away. It seemed like a long time, but it wasn't—not for building a derby car. First you had to find a sponsor to help out with expenses. Then you had to order a car kit from the International Derby Association. That got you started. The kit included drawings, patterns, and specifications, plus the axles and most of the hardware. You had to come up with the rest of your car parts yourself.

Ned's Hardware had agreed to sponsor Nicholas and Alex. They would chip in the money for the car kits, along with paint and brushes. But that still left helmets, wheels, wood, nails, tools, and whatever else they might need. And those things cost money.

"What about asking our dads to help out," said Nicholas.

"Sure," said Alex. "But you ask first."

"Why me?" asked Nicholas.

"Because then I can say, 'Nicholas's dad is giving him the money.' "

Nicholas sighed. "Thanks a lot," he said.

"It's okay," said Alex, grinning. "After all, what are best friends for?"

Nicholas wrapped his ankles around the rungs of his chair and speared a string bean with his fork. His little sister, Abbey, was feeding her dinner to the dog, and his mother had just burned a tray of biscuits. It probably wasn't the right moment to bring up the derby. But Nicholas knew that if he waited for the right moment, the race would be over.

"You know, Dad," he said, "the derby's just a few weeks off."

"That's right," said his father. "You and Alex ought to get started on your cars."

Nicholas nodded. "The trouble is," he said, "we're a little short of cash."

"I'd be glad to lend you some money," said his father, reaching for another helping of beans. "And you can pay me back."

"Pay you back?" said Nicholas.

"Isn't that what 'lend' means?"

"I guess so," said Nicholas, figuring how many allowances it would take to pay back the money.

"You know, Nicholas," said his father gently, "money doesn't grow on trees. I just bought you a new tire for your bicycle. And I thought you wanted a telescope for your birthday. What about your allowance?" Nicholas got three dollars a week for an allowance, more than any of his friends. But by the end of the week it always seemed to have disappeared. And worse, Nicholas could never really say what he spent it on. He was sure, though, that he hadn't bought anything that he didn't need. Pretty sure, anyway.

"When I was a boy," continued Nicholas's father, "I did odd jobs for money. I think it's about time you and Alex did something."

"You mean work?" Nicholas asked. "But we're only ten years old."

"That's right," said his father. "And that's old enough to take on a little responsibility."

"Responsibility," thought Nicholas. "So that's what being ten is all about."

Alex sat perched on his front steps, flipping through a stack of old comic books. He was agonizing over which ones to get rid of. His mother had accidentally come across the twelve piles he'd stashed in the back of his closet and declared them a fire hazard. "Parents!" he hissed.

"I'll say," said Nicholas, shuffling up the driveway.

"Well, how'd it go?" asked Alex. "Did you get the money?"

"Sort of."

"What do you mean 'sort of'?" Alex asked.

Nicholas broke the news slowly. If they wanted extra cash, they were going to have to work for it.

"Work?" said Alex.

"Yup," said Nicholas.

"Who's going to hire us?" asked Alex. "We're only ten years old."

2. Mrs. Peach to the Rescue

Word got around fast that there were two ten-year-olds willing to do odd jobs.

"And you thought no one would hire us," said Nicholas.

The trouble was, raking leaves took a lot of effort. So did mowing lawns and sweeping garages.

"There's got to be an easier way," said Nicholas, shoveling a pile of wet leaves into a large plastic bag.

That was when Mrs. Peach, Nicholas's next-door neighbor, telephoned. She was going to visit her daughter, who was having a baby, and she needed someone to look after Harry. Harry was her pet rabbit.

"Baby-sit?" Alex asked.

"Sure," said Nicholas. "Why not?"

"You remember when I baby-sat Annie?" said Alex. Annie was his little sister. "In ten short minutes she fell down the stairs, dumped an entire box of cookies into my aquarium, and threw up on my new tennis shoes."

"Annie's a baby," said Nicholas. "They're always trouble. How much trouble can a rabbit be?"

"Well," said Alex hesitantly, "I hope at least it's not a baby rabbit."

Mrs. Peach welcomed them with a firm handshake. She reminded Nicholas of his grandmother, round and sprightly. Her hair was the same funny blue-gray color, and she wore the same sensible shoes, with rubber soles that sent her bouncing with every step. She showed them into her bright, sunny kitchen and sat them down beside a plate of large chocolate wafers.

"She sure knows how to make a guy happy," whispered Alex. After they'd washed down a dozen with lemonade, she began asking questions. Did they have any pets? Had they ever baby-sat before?

"You understand," she said. "I don't want to leave Harry with just *anyone.*"

"Sure," said Nicholas. "We'll take good care of Harry. Don't worry."

"Now," she said, "I'm willing to pay you boys six dollars per week. How does that sound?"

It sounded too good to be true. Six dollars times five weeks. That was thirty dollars. "Wow," thought Nicholas.

Mrs. Peach led them to the backyard and introduced them to Harry.

"Harry," she said. Harry pricked up his tall pink ears. He sprang to his feet and sat back on his haunches. He was white and fat, and he had a brown spot in the middle of his belly. "I'd like you to meet Nicholas and Alex. They're going to look after you while I'm away." Harry narrowed his eyes and wrinkled his small pink nose. He looked at the boys nervously and then back at Mrs. Peach.

"Harry has a very specific routine," she said. "He doesn't like change."

She pulled a notebook from her hip pocket. "This is his menu," she said. "He eats at four, sharp, every day." Mrs. Peach had written out in bold letters a daily meal plan for Harry. On Monday, Wednesday, and Friday he ate carrots. On Tuesday and Thursday, lettuce.

On weekends he ate oatmeal. He drank two glasses of water a day and a pint of milk a week. She'd left plenty of food in the storage bin on the porch.

Mrs. Peach put aside the notebook and hauled a large green bag from under the steps. "Here are the wood shavings for his cage," she said. "It needs to be cleaned twice a week." She usually did it while Harry was exercising.

"Exercising?" Alex asked.

To the left of the porch was a small track surrounded by a white picket fence. Six small hurdles clutched the earth in a neat oval.

"Harry exercises every day just before dinner," she said. "Five times around the course."

Mrs. Peach then pointed to a tidy pile of magazines that lay in a basket beside the cage. "And he likes a story before bed. These are his favorites," she said, plucking three copies of *Reader's Digest* from the top of the pile.

Mrs. Peach lifted Harry from his cage and handed him, kicking and panting, to Nicholas. Nicholas stroked his head, and within seconds Harry was curled up in a ball on his lap.

"He likes me," said Nicholas triumphantly.

"I think you'll get along just fine," said Mrs. Peach.

3. Harry Has His Way

Alex bent over the split-rail fence that bounded the Buchanans' yard. He scooped up a smooth pebble lodged in the dirt and sent it skipping across the grass. "See," he said. "I knew it couldn't be as easy as it sounded."

"What's so hard about following a dumb schedule?" Nicholas asked. He was sitting on the fence, copying Harry's routine onto the back cover of his arithmetic book.

"She was pretty particular," said Alex.

"Who cares how particular she is?" said Nicholas. "Harry's the one who matters."

And Harry didn't seem too particular. He didn't seem to mind when they changed his exercise schedule to go to a baseball game, or when Nicholas began reading from a detective story.

"We're supposed to choose the books in the pile," Alex reminded him.

"He doesn't know what I'm reading. He's only a rabbit." Nicholas read one chapter, then put the book down. "Look," he said. Harry had closed his eyes just as he did when Nicholas read the *Reader's Digest.*

Harry didn't even seem to care when they fed him carrots on an oatmeal day, or when they forgot to refill his water bowl. But when Nicholas and Alex showed up one day two hours late for dinner, Harry was upset.

"Harry," said Nicholas. "Time for dinner. Eat your carrots like a good boy." But Harry wouldn't listen. He crept into a corner and began licking his hind paws.

"Okay," said Nicholas. "But you're not getting anything else." He flipped to chapter three of the detective story and began to read aloud. This time Harry wouldn't close his eyes. Instead, he began hopping from one end of his cage to the other. He upset his bowl of water and rolled over onto the pile of wet wood shavings.

"Harry," Nicholas cried. "You're making a

mess." He opened the cage and lifted Harry out. Harry dug his claws into Nicholas's chest.

"Ouch!" he cried as Harry jumped from his arms. Alex caught hold of him just as he was about to vault the fence. He set him down on the obstacle course.

"Let's see if this will calm you down," he said. Harry began his laps. He raced once around the track. On the second lap he stopped and turned around.

"Not that way, Harry!" cried Nicholas. But by that time Harry had hopped over the fence.

"Harry!" they called, chasing after him. "Harry, come back." But Harry kept right on running, across the lawn and into the meadow.

"He went that way," said Nicholas, pointing to a clump of bushes.

Alex knelt down and peered among the branches. He saw something white tangled

among them, but it didn't look like Harry. He reached in and pulled out an old sneaker. An hour later they'd come up with a flat bicycle tire, a roll of paper towels, and a dustpan, but no Harry.

"When he gets hungry," said Nicholas confidently, "he'll come back."

They cleaned Harry's cage and left a fresh carrot and a bowl of water. Next morning they stopped by Mrs. Peach's, but Harry hadn't returned. Two days later Harry still hadn't come back. By the end of the week it was clear that Harry wasn't coming back.

"So what are we going to tell the Peach?" said Alex. "If she comes home and Harry's gone . . ."

Nicholas had been thinking the same thing. Mrs. Peach would be furious. And Nicholas would have to face his mother and a lecture on responsibility. And of course, they wouldn't be paid.

"We could get a new rabbit," said Nicholas.

"Don't you think we're already in enough trouble?" asked Alex.

"Listen," Nicholas explained. "We'd get a rabbit that looks just like Harry. We could teach him Harry's routine, and the Peach would never know the difference."

"And what if Harry comes back?" asked Alex.

"You never were very good at math," said Nicholas.

"What does math have to do with Harry?" asked Alex.

"Two Harrys," said Nicholas, "are better than none. Right?"

Alex thought about it for a minute. "Right," he said.

4. Asking for Trouble

Nicholas and Alex stood at the counter of Pete's Pet Shop.

"What kind of a rabbit are you looking for?" asked Mr. Pete.

"Any kind," said Nicholas. "As long as it's fat and white with a brown spot on its belly."

Mr. Pete frowned and disappeared out back. He returned two minutes later holding a white fluffy rabbit. There in the middle of its belly was a brown spot just like the one Harry had.

"You're in luck," he said.

"How much?" Alex asked.

"Four dollars," said Mr. Pete.

Nicholas counted out four dollars while Mr. Pete tucked the rabbit into a cardboard box.

"Here you go," said Mr. Pete, handing the rabbit to Nicholas. Nicholas peered into an air hole in the top of the box.

"I hope you like your new home," he whispered.

"He'd better like his new home," said Alex.

Harry loved his new home. He liked the menu, and when Nicholas read from the *Reader's Digest,* he fell asleep just like the first Harry.

"Who wouldn't fall asleep," said Alex. "Listening to that stuff."

The only trouble were the hurdles. Harry would jump two and flop to a stop in front of the third.

"No, Harry," said Nicholas. "It's like this." Nicholas took two steps back and, with a flying leap, went sailing over the hurdles while Harry watched. Then Harry took two hops forward, flew over the first hurdle, and slid to a halt on his belly.

"Never mind," said Alex, reaching for one of Harry's carrots. "He'll catch on," he said, biting into it. Mrs. Peach wouldn't be back for four more weeks. That was plenty of time for Harry to feel right at home.

Three days later Harry stopped eating. He refused to exercise, and he whimpered when they read him the *Reader's Digest*. When Nicholas asked what was wrong, Harry looked up at him with big, sad eyes and began to glance about him as if he were looking for someone.

"I think he's lonely," said Alex.

"Maybe," said Nicholas, and he ran home to fetch Whiskers. Whiskers was his sister's stuffed rabbit. Nicholas set the bunny down in the grass next to Harry, who sniffed it and sent it toppling over with a furry paw. Alex sat the bunny back on its feet. But Harry tipped it over again.

"It's not going to work," said Alex. "He knows it's not real."

"Well, we can't get another rabbit," said Nicholas.

"That's for sure," said Alex. "But we'd better think of something before Mrs. Peach gets home."

They thought food might cheer Harry up, so they took him apples, cheese, cake, and ice cream. They read from all of the *Reader's Digest*s. Alex even brought along his favorite comic books. And when it was time for Harry to exercise, they removed half of the hurdles. But it was no use. Harry wasn't interested in food, in books, or in exercise.

"What's the matter with him?" complained Nicholas.

"I don't know," said Alex. "But I hope he's better soon."

5. Trouble Multiplies

Next day Harry felt much better. In fact, he looked very happy. Cuddled up next to him were twelve baby rabbits.

"Where did they come from?" cried Nicholas.

"It's pretty obvious," said Alex. "Harry had babies."

"You mean Harry's a *girl?*" asked Nicholas. "But we asked for a boy."

"No, we didn't," said Alex. "We asked for any rabbit as long as it was fat and white with a brown spot on its belly."

Nicholas was beginning to panic. "What are we going to do with twelve baby rabbits?"

The first thing to do was make a home for them. Harry's cage could barely hold Harry. It would never support a growing family of thirteen. Then they had to worry about feeding the rabbits. Harry would feed them for now, but when Mrs. Peach arrived home, they'd have to take over the care of the babies.

"We're going to have to hide them," said Alex.

"Where?" said Nicholas.

"Don't worry," said Alex, patting Nicholas on the back. "You'll figure something out."

That evening Mrs. Peach called. "I hope my Harry's not giving you any trouble," she said.

"He's not giving us any trouble at all," said Nicholas. After all, it was true. How could her Harry be trouble? They had no idea where he was.

"That's good news," said Mrs. Peach. But she had more news and it wasn't all good. Her daughter had had a nice healthy baby girl, and she'd be home a week earlier than she'd thought.

"Oh no!" cried Nicholas. "The Peach is coming home early!"

That called for emergency measures. If she came home and found Harry in this condition, she'd want to know the reason why. And they'd have to admit that they hadn't kept Harry on his schedule. She might even suspect that this wasn't her Harry.

"We've got to get Harry back in shape," said Alex. "Now that he—I mean, *she*—is thinner, maybe she will jump the hurdles."

They set Harry down on the track. She took three hops, paused, and slid to a stop in front of the first hurdle.

"Harry!" cried Nicholas.

"Think of the bright side," said Alex. "In a few weeks this will all be behind us, and we can start thinking about the derby."

"In a few weeks," thought Nicholas, "I might not be alive. If my mother finds out about these rabbits . . ." Nicholas had asked for a dog six months ago. He'd promised to feed it, exercise it, and take care of it. And he'd stuck to his promise, at least for the first two weeks. But after a while it seemed to Nicholas that it would be just as easy for his mother to take care of the dog.

"This is the last pet you'll have, Nicholas Buchanan," she'd said, "until you learn to be more responsible."

Nicholas felt very responsible now. Too responsible. He and Alex had twelve rabbits to look after, not counting Harry. They had to build a home for them, and soon they'd have to start feeding and exercising them. The trouble was that they still had to build their derby cars. Then there was school and homework, never mind baseball. They'd already missed three practices. Nicholas had told his coach that he had mumps, and Alex had called in sick with chicken pox. They were running out of childhood diseases. If only they could find someone who'd take the rabbits. They went to the pet shop and asked the owner if he wanted them.

"Sorry," he said, "I've got my hands full for another couple of months."

Then they put a sign up at school: RABBIT FAMILY FOR SALE. They tried selling the rabbits for fifty cents apiece.

When that didn't work, they changed their sign: RABBIT FAMILY FOR SALE—FREE!

But who wanted thirteen rabbits?

Nicholas thought of taking the rabbits to Alex's house and asking his sister to look after them. But Alex already had two dogs, two cats, sixteen goldfish, a turtle, and a baby alligator.

"No way," said Alex. "My mother said if I bring home one more animal, she'd put us all in the zoo."

6. Growing Pains

It took two full weeks to get Harry back in shape. She could jump all of the hurdles, but the trouble was the more she exercised, the more she ate. Harry was eating like a horse. She had already exhausted Mrs. Peach's supply of food, which meant that Nicholas had to break into his allowance. And pretty soon they'd have the babies to feed too.

"My mother is getting suspicious," Nicholas said. "I can't ask her to buy any more carrots. She's beginning to think I'm a rabbit."

"My dad's right when he says kids are expensive," said Alex.

"And they're a lot of trouble," said Nicholas, leafing through the *R* encyclopedia. "Here it is," he said. "Rabbit."

"What does it say?" asked Alex.

"It says baby rabbits leave the mother after about thirty days," said Nicholas, reading from the text. "It's only been three and a half weeks, but if we round off to the nearest week, then that's . . ."

"Four weeks," cried Alex.

"Exactly," said Nicholas.

They decided to move the babies to the barn in back of Nicholas's house. It was where they were planning to build their derby cars.

"Good thing we've got some lumber and nails," said Alex, digging into a pile of loose boards they'd put aside for their cars.

"Yeah," groaned Nicholas. "Too bad we have to use it for a new rabbit cage."

It took two full afternoons, most of the wood they'd saved for their cars, and all of the nails to build a new cage.

"What do you think?" asked Nicholas, admiring their work.

"I think it needs a few more nails," said Alex.

"It'll be all right," said Nicholas. "It's just temporary. After the derby we'll fix it up."

They anchored the cage to the floor of the

barn and filled it with wood shavings. Then
came the hard part—moving the babies. The
babies didn't want to leave Harry, and they
didn't want to leave each other. Every time
Nicholas tried to remove one from the cage,
the rest followed.

"They're like magnets!" he cried, struggling under a pile of furry feet.

"Drop them in here," said Alex, holding out the hood of his sweatshirt.

Nicholas dumped the rabbits into the hood three at a time, and Alex sprinted across the yard to the barn with them.

"You sure we've got them all?" he asked.

"I hope that's all of them," said Nicholas, pointing to Alex's sweatshirt. It was full of holes. "Swiss cheese," he said.

"It's better than Peach pie," said Alex, emptying the last batch of rabbits into the cage, "which is what we'd be if the Peach ever found out about this."

7. Welcome Home, Mrs. Peach

Mrs. Peach was arriving on the 9:30 p.m. plane. Nicholas and Alex would be in bed when she got home. But they wouldn't be sleeping. They were too worried about Harry. She certainly looked enough like the original Harry, but she didn't act like him. She ate more, she exercised less, and she slept most of the time. But the real problem was the sad, vacant look on her face. Harry wasn't happy, especially since they'd taken her babies away.

"Would your mother be happy," asked Alex, "if someone took you and Abbey away?"

"She'd be the happiest woman on earth," Nicholas had said. But he knew better. As much trouble as he was, Nicholas knew his mother really loved him and Abbey. She'd feel awful if someone took them away. Nicholas

thought how Harry must feel and breathed a
deep sigh. Maybe they should tell Mrs. Peach
the truth. At least then Harry could be with
her babies. They could always find another
rabbit for Mrs. Peach. Nicholas shut his eyes,
but he couldn't sleep. He tried counting sheep,
but they only turned into rabbits. Rabbits,
rabbits, everywhere.

Next morning, bright and early, Mrs. Peach
called to thank them for looking after Harry.
She said Harry must have had a good time
because he'd slept through breakfast.

"Harry's never done that before," she said,
sounding a bit worried.

She wanted Nicholas and Alex to stop by after school so she could pay them. And she thought maybe they might like to say hello to Harry. Alex thought it might be a good idea to take along a treat for Harry, so they stopped to pick up the latest issue of *Reader's Digest*.

"Here goes," said Nicholas. They walked up Mrs. Peach's driveway and rang the bell. Mrs. Peach came to the door wearing an emerald green dress and bright red lipstick. She'd swapped her sensible shoes for a pair of black pumps with tiny bows. She invited them in and led them out through the back to the patio, where Harry was. There were three small tables set with linen, cups, and saucers. Mrs. Peach was having some friends over for tea, to celebrate the birth of her new grand-daughter.

"Harry seems a bit tired," said Mrs. Peach, furrowing her brow. Nicholas walked over to the cage.

"Hi, Harry," he said. Harry widened her eyes. Then she jumped to her feet and began to hop straight up and down like a pogo stick.

"What's Harry doing?" asked Alex.

"Maybe he's just excited to see you," said Mrs. Peach nervously. But Harry was more than excited. She gritted her teeth and shivered.

"It's only me, Harry," said Nicholas. That upset Harry even more. She darted into a corner, covered her face, and whimpered.

"Perhaps I should never have left him," said Mrs. Peach, wringing her hands. "He's been acting so peculiar since I've been back. As if he didn't know me."

"Maybe it's the change," said Alex. "You said Harry didn't like change."

"Harry," said Mrs. Peach softly. She unlatched Harry's cage and reached in to pet her. Harry stopped whimpering. She narrowed her eyes, lowered her body, then sprang from the corner straight into Mrs. Peach's arms, knocking her to the ground.

"Harry," cried Mrs. Peach desperately. Harry hopped across the lawn and onto the obstacle course. Nicholas and Alex watched in astonishment as she began her laps followed by Mrs. Peach, who skipped over the hurdles crying, "Harry! Come back!" Suddenly Harry skidded to a stop. She sat on her haunches and drummed her paws against the ground.

"There, there," said Mrs. Peach, reaching out to grab Harry. Harry crept forward and jumped into Mrs. Peach's arms. Then she stretched her mouth into a broad grin and nipped Mrs. Peach on the thumb with her sharp white teeth.

"Ouch," cried Mrs. Peach, letting go of Harry. This time Harry bounded over the fence, into the meadow, and out of sight. Mrs. Peach collapsed into a chair, out of breath. Her blue hair had tumbled down around her face, and her fine blue veins stood out. Her lipstick was smeared and her green dress was covered with dust. She looked old and frail. "It's no use," she said with tears in her eyes. "I've lost my Harry. It's my fault. I should never have left him. He forgot all about me."

Nicholas had tears in his eyes too. Alex had gone into the kitchen for a tissue. He handed it to Mrs. Peach. "Are you okay?" he asked.

Mrs. Peach nodded, sobbing. She reached for her handbag. She was going to pay them.

"After all," she said. "I'm sure you tried."

"But we didn't," Nicholas blurted out. "It's our fault. That wasn't Harry. At least, it wasn't *your* Harry." Then the whole story spilled out of how they'd let the first Harry get away and

how they'd bought another rabbit to take his place.

"We're really sorry," said Alex.

"We'll get you another rabbit," said Nicholas.

Mrs. Peach rocked back and forth in her chair. She wiped her nose and looked from Nicholas to Alex. She wore the same vacant expression that Harry had had.

"I wish she'd just get mad at us," Nicholas thought. But she didn't. Instead, she became very still. She took her purse from her lap and placed it back on the table. Of course she wasn't going to pay them now. She looked at Harry's empty cage with the door flapping on its hinges. Nicholas guessed she wanted them to go.

"Good-bye, Mrs. Peach," he said softly, and they quietly walked away.

"She must have really loved that rabbit," said Alex.

"If we'd only stuck to his schedule," said Nicholas, "then none of this would have happened."

8. Surprise! Surprise!

Nicholas felt terrible about what had happened. But he felt positively sick to his stomach when he thought about what would happen when their parents found out about Harry and the baby rabbits. And they were bound to find out sooner or later.

"The worst my parents can do," said Alex, "is put me in the zoo."

"I'd rather be put in the zoo than miss the derby," said Nicholas. He was sure that when his parents found out about the rabbits, they wouldn't let him race. Even if they did, he had no money for spare parts to finish his car.

"Well," said Nicholas, "we might as well get it over with now." He said good-bye to Alex and started home. His mother had left a note on the kitchen table. She'd gone to the bank but would be back in an hour.

"One more hour to live," said Nicholas, throwing himself across his bed.

Suddenly he heard the kitchen door slam. His mother was back.

Nicholas rolled off the bed and slid down the banister.

"Nicholas Buchanan," called his mother from the kitchen. "I've told you a hundred times not to slide down that banister."

"That's for sure," said Nicholas. "Maybe two hundred." He hopped off the railing and wandered into the kitchen. His mother was sorting through the mail. Nicholas was just about to say something about the rabbits when his mother handed him a letter.

"For you," she said. Nicholas opened it. It was from his grandmother, and inside was a birthday card and a check.

"Twenty-five dollars!" cried Nicholas, forgetting all about Harry and the baby rabbits. "It's a miracle!"

"I wouldn't call it a miracle," said his mother. "But it's a nice surprise."

"I'll say," said Nicholas, racing to the upstairs phone. He'd better tell Alex before Alex told his parents about the rabbits. Twenty-five dollars was plenty for spare parts for both of them.

"Great!" said Alex. "But we're going to have to tell our parents sometime."

"Right," said Nicholas. "But if we tell them now, we might not get to race. If we tell them later, the race will be over. Got it?"

"Got it," said Alex.

"Besides," said Nicholas, "it's just for another few weeks. The rabbits will be safe and sound in the barn until then."

Nicholas hung up the phone. He jumped on his bed and began to think about the derby. He and Alex had to start building their cars. The race was just three weeks away.

"Three weeks," echoed Nicholas's mother from down the hall.

"What is she, a mind reader?" thought Nicholas, rolling over onto his stomach. "Three weeks till what?" he asked.

"Three weeks until the rummage sale," said his mother, flying past the bedroom door. "I've got to get that barn cleaned out."

"What barn?" asked Nicholas, springing up from the bed.

"That barn," said Mrs. Buchanan, pointing across the yard and hauling the pail and broom out of the cleaning closet.

"But you can't!" cried Nicholas.

Nicholas's mother eyed him suspiciously. "What do you mean I can't?" she asked.

Nicholas had to think fast. "Alex and I wanted to do it," he explained.

"You *wanted* to do it?" Nicholas's mother asked with raised eyebrows. "Since when?"

"Since we started doing odd jobs," said Nicholas.

"I see," said Nicholas's mother, smiling. "So you're going to charge me for it."

"Just five dollars," said Nicholas weakly. He knew the job was worth more, but he didn't want to risk having his mother say no.

"How about eight?" said his mother.

"Seven," said Nicholas, feeling guilty.

"It's a deal," said his mother.

Nicholas stacked the broom and cleaning supplies neatly in a corner. Then he carefully began to pry the rabbit cage loose from the barn floor. His mother had gotten the bright idea of inspecting the barn after they'd cleaned it. That meant they had to move the rabbits again.

"Just when we thought our troubles were over," said Nicholas.

"Where are we going to put them?" Alex asked.

"In the storeroom," said Nicholas. "Off the kitchen."

"You mean we're moving them into the house!" cried Alex.

"It's just for a few hours," said Nicholas. "No one will notice."

Nicholas handed the cage to Alex. "When you see her coming," he said, "cut around the other side of the barn."

Alex nodded and bent over to tie his shoelaces. Nicholas posted himself at the window.

"Here she comes," he cried. Alex clutched the sides of the rabbit cage and slipped out the door. The storeroom was easy enough to find. It was filled with everything from cardboard boxes to bicycle tires.

"Nicholas is right," thought Alex. "Who's

going to notice a few rabbits with all this junk." He covered the cage with a dark cloth and set it inside a large cardboard box. He placed the box high on top of a pile of luggage and dashed back to the barn. Nicholas's mother was just leaving.

"Good work, Alex," she said.

"Yeah," said Nicholas, winking, "good work."

"Now all we have to do is wait for your mother to go out," said Alex.

They waited all afternoon, the next morning, and half of the next afternoon. But Nicholas's mother didn't budge from the house.

"I don't understand," said Nicholas, who had slipped into the storeroom with a bowl of fresh water and some shredded lettuce. "It's the first time in my whole life that my mother has stayed inside for two whole days."

"I hope she doesn't smell trouble," said Alex, who was standing guard at the door.

"She's going to smell trouble," said Nicholas, "if we don't get these rabbits out of here or at least clean the cage."

"What if your mother never goes out of the house again?"

"She has a dentist's appointment the day after tomorrow," said Nicholas. "She'll have to go out then."

"What about tomorrow?" asked Alex.

"She'll be home tomorrow. It's my birthday," said Nicholas. "Remember?"

"That's right," said Alex. "We ought to be celebrating."

"You mean instead of worrying," said Nicholas.

9. Nicholas Has a Birthday

Nicholas lay in bed staring at the ceiling. He was ten years old. He'd been waiting all year for this day. Now he wished he could roll over in bed and forget all about it, but that was impossible. At seven Abbey awakened him by blowing a noisemaker in his ear. Then, when he went downstairs, he found his mother in the kitchen humming "Happy Birthday" and preparing a mountain of food. And the living room and dining room were off-limits.

"What's going on?" asked Nicholas.

"I'm making your favorite sandwiches," said his mother. "Peanut butter and banana." Nicholas's mouth began to water.

"How about one now?" he asked. Nicholas grabbed a sandwich and escaped to the porch. He was just going back for another when his mother hollered, "Nicholas!"

"Yeah, Mom," Nicholas answered.

"Would you mind running to the store for a quart of milk?" she asked.

"Now?" said Nicholas. The truth was, he did mind. What if she found the rabbits while he was gone? Why couldn't *she* go to the store? Then he could move the rabbits back to the barn.

"If you want brownies for lunch," said his mother, "I have to have some milk."

"Okay," said Nicholas grudgingly. He took his bicycle hoping to save time, but it took forever. First he had to wait for the man from the dairy to unload the milk. Then he stood for twenty minutes at the checkout counter. By the time he got home it was past noon.

"Mom!" Nicholas cried, setting the milk down on the kitchen table. But there was no answer.

Nicholas looked upstairs. He checked the backyard and the basement. "Where is everyone?" he said. He passed the dining room and stopped in front of the closed doors. He turned the knob to peek in.

"Surprise! Surprise!" Standing around the table was half of Nicholas's fourth-grade class.

"Happy birthday," said Nicholas's mother, planting a big kiss on his cheek.

"Gee!" said Nicholas. His mother had decorated the room with balloons and streamers, and the table was piled high with cookies, brownies, sandwiches, and punch. In a corner was a stack of presents. Nicholas sat down at the head of the table. He picked up a party favor and blew as hard as he could.

"Does that mean we can start eating?" asked Alex.

"You bet," said Nicholas's mother. She began to pass around the sandwiches and serve the punch while Nicholas opened presents. There were games, records, a telescope from his parents, and a book and a rabbit's foot from Alex.

"For good luck," said Alex. Nicholas laughed and hooked the foot to his belt. He'd forgotten all about the rabbits, and he didn't want to start thinking about them now. He piled his plate with cookies and peanut butter sandwiches and dug in.

"All right," said Nicholas's mother when everyone had finished eating, "everybody into the living room."

"What about the cake?" Alex wanted to know.

"First I want to introduce you all to Walter," said Nicholas's mother. Standing in the middle of the living room was a tall man in black. He looked like a magician.

"Ladies and gentlemen," said Walter. "Good afternoon." He bowed and introduced his lovely assistant, Rose. Rose curtsied and took her place behind a long table covered in black.

The magician asked everyone to sit down. Then he asked Nicholas's mother to step forward. He tugged on his black tie, and it blossomed into a bunch of flowers.

"For you, madam," he said, bowing gracefully. Next the magician asked for a volunteer. Alex's sister raised her hand, and the magician ushered her into a tall narrow box. He closed it tight and counted to three. When he reopened the box, she'd disappeared.

"Bring her back!" cried someone.

"All right," said the magician. He pulled the day's paper from his back pocket and rolled it into a tube. He whispered softly and the lights went out. The paper burst into ten flaming candles, and in marched Alex's sister with a huge chocolate cake. Everyone applauded and broke into a chorus of "Happy Birthday" while Nicholas's mother cut the cake. Suddenly, the magician removed his hat. He tossed it into the air, tapped it three times, and set it squarely on the black table.

"Mumbo jumbo," said the magician, stretching his hand deep into the hat. Out it came, holding a small white rabbit.

"That's all we need," said Nicholas. "Another rabbit."

The magician looked at the rabbit and blinked. He rubbed his eyes and peered into the hat again. Out popped another rabbit onto the black table. Then another and another.

"More! More!" shouted Nicholas's friends, and the more they cried, the more rabbits hopped out of the hat. Soon there were twelve little rabbits bounding across the living room, heading straight for the cake. One rabbit was about to nosedive straight into the frosting when Alex caught hold of its feet.

"Hey," whispered Alex. "These look like Harry's babies."

"What!" cried Nicholas, lifting the cake into the air.

"No!" cried Nicholas's mother as one of the rabbits bumped against her favorite lamp. She looked sternly at the magician. "What's going on here?" she scolded. "You should know better than to let a dozen rabbits loose in my living room. You told me you had just one rabbit."

"I do," said the magician, glaring at Rose, "and I'd like to know where it is."

By now Rose had climbed onto a chair. "I don't know what happened," she said. "I took the box from the storeroom just like you asked."

"The storeroom!" cried Alex.

"The storeroom!" echoed Nicholas's mother, turning pale.

"Yes," said the magician. "That's where I left the rabbit for my act." He marched into the kitchen and opened the door to the storeroom. Sure enough, in the corner was a box and inside was a large white rabbit. "Here he is," said the magician, smiling.

"Wait a minute!" cried Nicholas's mother.

"That's not your rabbit," she said. "That's *my* rabbit."

"*Your* rabbit!" Nicholas choked. "What are you doing with a rabbit?"

"Mr. Purdie, the vet, found it sitting on his step one morning, and we said we'd take it. After we saw what a good time you had looking after Mrs. Peach's rabbit, we thought it would make a great birthday present."

Nicholas looked closely at the rabbit. Something about it looked awfully familiar. "Isn't this our Harry?" he said to Alex.

Alex nodded. "I was just thinking the same thing," he said.

Meanwhile, the magician had stepped over a pile of luggage. "Here's my rabbit," he said, lifting another box from deep in the corner. "Here's my baby." He reached inside and pulled out another large white rabbit.

Suddenly Alex cried, "It's Harry. Mrs. Peach's Harry!"

"Harry!" cried the magician.

"Mrs. Peach!" cried Nicholas's mother, who was by now fully confused.

"That rabbit belongs to Mrs. Peach," explained Nicholas. "And we have to give him back."

"This rabbit belongs to me," said the magician angrily. "It's the only rabbit I have."

"What about all those rabbits?" said Nicholas's mother, pointing to the living room.

"Those aren't my rabbits," said the magician.

"Well, then whose are they?" cried Nicholas's mother. "Would someone explain to me what's going on here!"

"It's a long story," said Nicholas.

"Wait!" cried Alex, interrupting. He turned to the magician. "We'll give you all of those rabbits," he said, pointing to Harry's babies, "if you'll give us Harry."

At first the magician looked skeptical. Then he peered into the living room. "They certainly were a success," he said.

"It's a deal then?" asked Alex.

"It's a deal," said the magician.

Nicholas's mother stood with her hands on her hips, shaking her head. "All right," she said, "I don't know who any of these rabbits belong to anymore, and I don't care. But if they're not out of my house in five minutes, all of you will be out of the house."

"Hear that?" said Nicholas, turning to his friends. "Everyone grab a rabbit!" It took longer than five minutes, but they finally cornered all of the rabbits and returned them to the cage.

"Is that all of them?" asked Alex.

"An even dozen," said the magician, closing the door.

"Good," said Alex, wiping his brow. "You know what I'm ready for? A nice big slice of cake."

10. Welcome Home, Harry

Nicholas and Alex started up the path with Harry to Mrs. Peach's house.

"Well," said Alex, "now that this is over with, we can start thinking about the derby."

"The funny thing is," said Nicholas, "the derby doesn't seem so important anymore. At least winning doesn't. What really feels important is getting Harry back."

"Yeah," said Alex, tickling Harry's paw. "Losing a race couldn't be half as bad as losing Harry."

"You know something," said Nicholas. "I think I'm going to name my derby car Harry."

"Great idea," said Alex, mounting Mrs. Peach's front steps. "And I can call mine the Peach."

Nicholas rang the bell. Mrs. Peach opened the door a crack and peeked out.

"Thank you," she said. "But I'm not interested in another rabbit."

"But this isn't another rabbit!" cried Nicholas. "It's Harry. *Your* Harry." Nicholas lifted Harry's face up to the door. Mrs. Peach opened it a bit wider. Her eyes began to sparkle, and her long, thin mouth stretched into a wide grin. Suddenly she looked ten years younger. "Why, it really is Harry!" she said, and she gathered him from Nicholas's arms.

"Welcome home, Harry!" she cried, giving him a huge kiss. "Where have you been, you naughty boy?" She turned to Nicholas and Alex. "Where did you find him?" she asked.

"I guess you could say he found us," said Alex, smiling.

They followed Mrs. Peach into the backyard and watched her put Harry back into his cage. He settled into a corner, closed his eyes, and took a deep breath. He was happy to be home. Mrs. Peach pulled a menu from her side pocket. It was almost four o'clock, and it was an oatmeal day. Harry nibbled on his dinner, drank a bowl of water, and stretched himself out.

"He's tired," said Mrs. Peach. "I guess it's been a long day."

"I'll say," said Nicholas. He and Alex said good night to Harry. Then they said good-bye to Mrs. Peach and started home.

"Now," said Nicholas, "I have to feed *my* Harry." He reached into the kitchen cupboard for a bowl and filled it with shredded lettuce. "Today," he said, heading for the barn, "will be a lettuce day." He set the bowl down in front of Harry. Harry blinked and began nibbling the lettuce. When she finished, she rolled over onto her side and looked at Nicholas. Then she closed her eyes.

"Looks like she's ready for bed," said Nicholas.

"What about a story," said Alex. "She has to have a story."

"That's right," said Nicholas. "What are we going to read to her?"

Alex reached into his jacket pocket. "How about this?" he said. It was the very latest edition of *Reader's Digest*. Alex thumbed through the pages and began to read aloud.

"Boy," said Nicholas, yawning, "you really know how to put a guy to sleep."

"I don't know about that," said Alex, who was looking at Harry. Harry was curled up in a tiny ball with her eyes tightly shut. "But I sure know how to put a rabbit to sleep."

About the Author

KATE BANKS has always wanted a pet rabbit. When she was eight years old, she sent away for a "backyard rabbit," which came in a choice of black, white, brown, or gray. "Six weeks later it arrived," she says, "a flat, white, twelve-inch wooden rabbit with pink ears, to be used as a garden prop. I was so disappointed."

Kate is the author of two picture books, *Alphabet Soup,* illustrated by Peter Sis, and *Big, Bigger, Biggest Adventure,* illustrated by Paul Yalowitz. She lives with her husband in Italy.

About the Illustrator

BLANCHE SIMS had many pets as a child. "Animals are so much fun to draw," she says. "They have great personalities. Some are beautiful to watch, and others are really goofy. I once had a baby chick who would ride on the back of my collie."

Blanche has illustrated many books for children, including *Soccer Sam, Cannonball Chris, Red Ribbon Rosie,* and *The Pizza Pie Slugger.* She lives in Connecticut.

D0651116

G
Editor-in-chief

NEW DIRECTIONS FOR YOUTH DEVELOPMENT

Theory
Practice
Research

summer | 2006

The Case for Twenty-First Century Learning

Eric Schwarz
Ken Kay

issue
editors

JOSSEY-BASS™
An Imprint of
⊕WILEY

The Case for Twenty-First Century Learning
Eric Schwarz, Ken Kay (eds.)
New Directions for Youth Development, No. 110, Summer 2006
Gil G. Noam, Editor-in-Chief

Microfilm copies of issues and articles are available in 16mm and 35mm, as well as microfiche in 105mm, through University Microfilms Inc., 300 North Zeeb Road, Ann Arbor, Michigan 48106-1346.

New Directions for Youth Development (ISSN 1533-8916, electronic ISSN 1537-5781) is part of The Jossey-Bass Psychology Series and is published quarterly by Wiley Subscription Services, Inc., A Wiley Company, at Jossey-Bass, 989 Market Street, San Francisco, California 94103-1741. POSTMASTER: Send address changes to New Directions for Youth Development, Jossey-Bass, 989 Market Street, San Francisco, California 94103-1741.

Subscriptions cost $80.00 for individuals and $180.00 for institutions, agencies, and libraries. Prices subject to change. Refer to the order form at the back of this issue.

Editorial correspondence should be sent to the Editor-in-Chief, Dr. Gil G. Noam, McLean Hospital, 115 Mill Street, Belmont, MA 02478.

Cover photograph by Age Fotostock

www.josseybass.com

Contents

Issue Editors' Notes

AS THE DEBATE OVER education reform continues in the United States, we seem to have reached concurrence on a few basic points:

- American students are not performing well in comparison to many of their foreign counterparts.[1]
- American high schools in their present form are obsolete.[2]
- American schools are seeming less and less relevant to American students.
- The American public is keenly aware of the need to equip students with a set of skills beyond the basics in order for them to succeed in the new twenty-first century global economy.[3]

But there remain two important holes in our current thinking that need to be broadly addressed:

- We have not come to closure on the new skill set students need to succeed as twenty-first century citizens and workers.
- We have not been clear that we need a new broad alliance of schools and other community-based youth groups to work together to promote and implement this new learning agenda.

This volume invited by Gil Noam, editor-in-chief of *New Directions for Youth Development*, addresses these two gaps in our current consensus and in our view promotes forcefully a skills agenda that traditional education and newer youth development groups can jointly embrace to create a new momentum for education in our nation's communities.

NEW DIRECTIONS FOR YOUTH DEVELOPMENT, NO. 110, SUMMER 2006 © WILEY PERIODICALS, INC.
Published online in Wiley InterScience (www.interscience.wiley.com) • DOI: 10.1002/yd.161

The rationale

While much has been written about our current education land-scape, a few facts bear repeating:

- The United States is falling behind on critical international comparisons of educational performance. On the 2003 Programme for International Student Assessment exam in mathematics, U.S. fifteen-year-old students ranked twenty-fourth out of twenty-nine countries that belong to the Organisation for Economic Cooperation and Development. The U.S. ranking in problem solving in practical, real-world situations, which goes beyond the mastery of mathematics techniques conventionally taught in U.S. schools, was tied with Spain, Portugal, and Italy and ahead of only Greece, Turkey, and Mexico. American students ranked well behind students in the highest-performing countries: Finland, Japan, and Korea.
- The proportion of the college-age population that earned degrees in science and engineering fields, which are indispensable to economic growth, were substantially larger in more than sixteen countries in Asia and Europe than in the United States in 2000, according to the National Science Board's 2004 *Science and Engineering Indicators Report.*[4]
- There are wide gaps between the skills that businesses value and the skills most graduates actually have. For example, 80 percent of employers in the fastest-growing industries assess writing as part of the hiring process, according to a 2004 report of the National Commission on Writing in America's Schools and Colleges.[5] Yet more than 75 percent of twelfth graders are not proficient in writing, according to the 2002 National Assessment of Academic Progress.

In short, other nations are recognizing the critical value of the skills that matter in the twenty-first century while the United States has allowed itself to fall behind. We are in a global competition, in which many countries are off and running to excel in the new relevant skill sets, while the United States is still using old models and old metrics.

New directions toward twenty-first century learning

This situation requires a national conversation on the skills children need to succeed in the twenty-first century and the venues where they can develop them—in school and out of school. We need a willingness to focus on those skills as the outcomes of learning and the best assets young people have in being successful workers and citizens.

The framework offered by the Partnership for 21st Century Skills, America's leading advocacy organization focused on infusing twenty-first century skills into education, suggests that our current focus on core subjects mastery needs to be complemented by four other significant components:

- Thinking and learning skills (critical thinking and problem solving, creativity and innovation, communication, and collaboration skills)
- Information and communication technology literacy (the ability to accomplish thinking and learning skills through the use of technology)
- Life skills (leadership, ethics, personal productivity, self-directed learning)
- Twenty-first century content (global awareness and business fundamentals and economic literacy)

These are the skills and subjects that are not adequately focused on today in our educational system, but are the skills our national business and education leaders have identified as being central to the success of students as twenty-first century citizens and workers.

Citizen Schools, a leading national education initiative that helps improve student achievement by blending real-world learning and rigorous academics after school, is leading a movement to reimagine after-school education, where quality after-school programs become full partners with schools in learning. Afterschool offers the opportunity

NEW DIRECTIONS FOR YOUTH DEVELOPMENT • DOI: 10.1002/yd

of not only more time but also more actual hands-on experiences and more people involved in young people's lives. All of these resources, when well integrated with rigorous in-school academics and projects, can help students develop mastery in twenty-first century skills.

The new conversation

Twenty-first century learning frames an increasingly relevant and vital national conversation about what we are collectively trying to help young people achieve: the skills and attributes that will allow them to succeed in the new global economy. A focus on outcomes such as critical thinking, problem solving, innovation, and communications skills can create a new focus for students, parents, educators, and policymakers on the specific outcomes we need young people to strive for and help them attain. This can lead to a broader conversation within each community about all of the individuals and groups that can play a role in helping young people attain twenty-first century skills.

Problem solving, creativity, leadership, and ethics are in the domain of every institution within a community that touches youth development, not just K–12 institutions. The skills conversation is a new opportunity for all of these groups to come together with traditional K–12 education and identify a comprehensive strategy to address the full panoply of twenty-first century skills in each community.

The chapters in this volume provide a broad scope of perspectives on the need, opportunity, application, and outcomes of twenty-first century learning and therefore provide a helpful backdrop for these new conversations. They make the case that the United States needs to redefine educational success, embrace twenty-first century skills, and offer perspectives on how some schools and programs can and are doing this.

To make the case for twenty-first century learning, Michael Dell and Karen Bruett in Chapter One and Allyson Knox in Chapter Two explain in principle and in practice why business in the modern economy demands twenty-first century skills. Michele Sacconaghi in Chapter Three reveals broad public support for a "basics-plus" education that better integrates twenty-first century skills in learning and youth development. In Chapter Four, Blenda Wilson demonstrates how vital learning in school and in after-school programs is for closing the achievement gap in the United States. Frank Levy and Richard Murnane provide in Chapter Five an analysis of how the nation's educational system can and must be changed in order to fit the nature and needs of the twenty-first century economy and citizenry.

To create an agenda for the research and practice of twenty-first century learning, Ken Kay and Margaret Honey outline in Chapter Six the framework for twenty-first century skills, along with their definition and measurement. In Chapter Seven, Eric Schwarz and David Stolow demonstrate the unique advantages of out-of-school time as a venue for the kinds of real-world experiences and civic engagement that enable young people to develop a broad, well-rounded package of skills.

In showing the wide-ranging application of twenty-first century skills, Bob Pearlman describes in Chapter Eight an innovative approach to project-based learning and twenty-first century skills outcomes in a model high school. In Chapter Nine, Marcia Capuano and Troy Knoderer explain how their pioneering professional development and assessment systems speak to learning in the digital age. David Driscoll paints a picture in Chapter Ten of how states need to and can refocus education systems toward learning for greater economic competitiveness. Cathann Kress in Chapter Eleven and John Box in Chapter Twelve show how their programs (respectively, National 4-H and Junior Achievement) have developed a long-standing tradition of and are innovatively pushing forward with twenty-first century learning in the after-school sector. In Chapter Thirteen, John Wilson discusses the importance and necessity that teachers give to twenty-first century skills and how they can be supported in incorporating those skills into the classroom. Finally, in Chapter Fourteen, Leidi Cabral, a high school student at Boston Latin School, draws from her experience as a young learner to describe the power of twenty-first century learning in helping make her a success now and in the future.

NEW DIRECTIONS FOR YOUTH DEVELOPMENT • DOI: 10.1002/yd

Reimagine learning

A wonderful group of people greatly aided all of us in putting together this volume of *New Directions for Youth Development*. We especially thank Mary Buckley and Maureen Cain from the Partnership for 21st Century Skills; Jason Cascarino, Adrian K. Haugabrook, and Katie Perry from Citizen Schools; and Erin Cooney and Gil Noam from Harvard University and the Program in Education, Afterschool and Resilience (PEAR).

We believe this volume of *New Directions for Youth Development* fills a void in our national education debate. As the chapter authors collectively argue, we need to reimagine the learning day—building partnerships that engage schools, after-school programs, businesses, and community-based organizations—and embrace both traditional academic basics as well as small-group and project-based learning that will give students a chance to master twenty-first century skills. By focusing on twenty-first century outcomes for our young people and the broad alliance that needs to work toward them, we can potentially take our national education debates in the new directions in which they urgently need to go.

Notes

1. See the latest National Assessment for Educational Progress, Programme for International Student Assessment, and Trends in Mathematics and Science Study.

2. Gates, B. (2005, February 26). Remarks presented at the National Education Summit on High Schools, Washington, D.C.

3. Time Warner Foundation. (2003, June). *Twenty-first century literacy: A vital component in learning*. Survey conducted by Lake Snell Perry & Associates and Market Strategies. New York: Time Warner Foundation.

4. "Science and engineering indicators 2004." National Science Board, 2004. http://www.nsf.gov/statistics/seind04/pdfstart.htm

5. National Commission on Writing for America's Families, Schools, and Colleges. (2004, September). *Writing: A ticket to work . . . or a ticket out: A survey of business leaders*. Report. New York: College Board.

Eric Schwarz
Ken Kay
Editors

ERIC SCHWARZ *is president and CEO of Citizen Schools, a leading national education initiative that helps improve student achievement by blending real-world learning and rigorous academics after school.*

KEN KAY *is president of the Partnership for 21st Century Skills, America's leading advocacy organization focused on infusing twenty-first century skills into education.*

Executive Summary

Chapter One: *Why American business demands twenty-first century skills: An industry perspective*

Karen Bruett

Public education is the key to individual and business prosperity. With a vested stake in education, educators, employers, parents, policymakers, and the public should question how this nation's public education system is faring. Knowing that recent international assessments have shown little or no gains in American students' achievement, the author asserts the clear need for change.

As both a large American corporate employer and a provider of technology for schools, Dell is concerned with ensuring that youth will thrive in their adult lives. Changing workplace expectations lead to a new list of skills students will need to acquire before completing their schooling. Through technology, Dell supports schools in meeting educational goals, striving to supply students with the necessary skills, referred to as twenty-first century skills.

The Partnership for 21st Century Skills, of which Dell is a member, has led an initiative to define what twenty-first century learning should entail. Through extensive research, the partnership has built a framework outlining twenty-first century skills: analytical thinking, communication, collaboration, global awareness, and technological and economic literacy. Dell and the partnership are

WILEY InterScience®
DISCOVER SOMETHING GREAT

NEW DIRECTIONS FOR YOUTH DEVELOPMENT, NO. 110, SUMMER 2006 © WILEY PERIODICALS, INC.
Published online in Wiley InterScience (www.interscience.wiley.com) • DOI: 10.1002/yd.162

working state by state to promote the integration of these skills into curricula, professional development for teachers, and classroom environments. The authors describe two current initiatives, one in Virginia, the other in Texas, which both use technology to help student learning.

All stakeholders can take part in preparing young people to compete in the global economy. Educators and administrators, legislators, parents, and employers must play their role in helping students be ready for what the workforce and the world has in store for them.

Chapter Two: Why American business demands twenty-first century learning: A company perspective

Allyson Knox

Microsoft is an innovative corporation demonstrating the kind and caliber of job skills needed in the twenty-first century. It demonstrates its commitment to twenty-first century skills by holding its employees accountable to a set of core competencies, enabling the company to run effectively. The author explores how Microsoft's core competencies parallel the Partnership for 21st Century Skills learning frameworks. Both require advanced problem-solving skills and a passion for technology, both expect individuals to be able to work in teams, both look for a love of learning, and both call for the self-confidence to honestly self-evaluate.

Microsoft also works to cultivate twenty-first century skills among future workers, investing in education to help prepare young people for competitive futures. As the need for digital literacy has become imperative, technology companies have taken the lead in facilitating technology training by partnering with schools and communities. Microsoft is playing a direct role in preparing students for what lies ahead in their careers.

To further twenty-first century skills, or core competencies, among the nation's youth, Microsoft has established Partners in Learning, a program that helps education organizations build partnerships that leverage technology to improve teaching and learn-

NEW DIRECTIONS FOR YOUTH DEVELOPMENT • DOI: 10.1002/yd

ing. One Partners in Learning grantee is Global Kids, a nonprofit organization that trains students to design online games focused on global social issues resonating with civic and global competencies. As Microsoft believes the challenges of competing in today's economy and teaching today's students are substantial but not insurmountable, such partnerships and investments demonstrate Microsoft's belief in and commitment to twenty-first century skills.

Chapter Three: Why the American public supports twenty-first century learning

Michele Sacconaghi

Aware that constituent support is essential to any educational endeavor, the AOL Time Warner Foundation (now the Time Warner Foundation), in conjunction with two respected national research firms, measured Americans' attitudes toward the implementation of twenty-first century skills. The foundation's national research survey was intended to explore public perceptions of the need for changes in the educational system, in school and after school, with respect to the teaching of twenty-first century skills. The author summarizes the findings of the survey, which were released by the foundation in June 2003.

One thousand adults were surveyed by telephone, including African Americans, Latinos, teachers, and business executives. In general, the survey found that Americans believe today's students need a "basics-plus" education, meaning communication, technology, and critical thinking skills in addition to the traditional basics of reading, writing, and math. In fact, 92 percent of respondents stated that students today need different skills from those of ten to twenty years ago. Also, after-school programs were found to be an appropriate vehicle to teach these skills. Furthermore, the survey explored how well the public perceives schools to be preparing youth for the workforce and postsecondary education, which twenty-first century skills are seen as being taught effectively, and the level of need for after-school and summer programs.

The survey results provide conclusive evidence of national support for basics-plus education. Thus, a clear opportunity exists to build momentum for a new model of education for the twenty-first century.

Chapter Four: Why America's disadvantaged communities need twenty-first century learning

Blenda J. Wilson

Current school reform efforts, emphasizing data and accountability, have shed additional light on racial and income-based inequities in education. To tackle this achievement gap, the discrepancies in the nation's educational system must be examined within the context of the increasing economic demand for higher skill levels. The author asserts that the education system is not educating all students to the levels necessary to fulfill America's quest for international excellence.

Demonstrating the inadequacies of the current educational system, this chapter draws from Murnane and Levy's research emphasizing a need for new basic skills. The author cites Murnane and Levy's finding that up to half of all graduates leave high school without the skills necessary to compete in today's economy. Students are not getting enough out of school to succeed in the workforce.

These data prompt the author's support for out-of-school-time programs. An opportunity gap exists when it comes to how children from various socioeconomic backgrounds spend their out-of-school time. Children from disadvantaged families experience much less enrichment, further contributing to the achievement gap. Quality after-school programs—not just "more school"—can fill this void, providing the enrichment and academic support needed to gain the skills required to succeed in the modern workforce. The Nellie Mae Education Foundation's Critical Hours: Afterschool Programs and Educational Success confirms the need for out-of-school-time programs by showing the relationship between an

NEW DIRECTIONS FOR YOUTH DEVELOPMENT • DOI: 10.1002/yd

effective after-school program and academic success. Ultimately the after-school movement will reduce educational inequality, allowing today's youth to contribute to America's international competitiveness.

Chapter Five: Why the changing American economy calls for twenty-first century learning: Answers to educators' questions

Frank Levy, Richard J. Murnane

While struggling with the current pressures of educational reform, some educators will ask whether their efforts make economic sense. Questioning the future makeup of the nation's workforce, many wonder how the educational system should be tempered to better prepare today's youth. This chapter answers educators' and parents' questions around the effect of fluctuations in the American economy on the future of education. The authors offer reassurance that good jobs will always be available, but warn that those jobs will require a new level of skills: expert thinking and complex communication. Schools need to go beyond their current curriculum and prepare students to use reading, math, and communication skills to build a deeper and more thoughtful understanding of subject matter.

To explain the implications of the nation's changing economy on jobs, technology, and therefore education, the authors address a range of vital questions. Citing occupational distribution data, the chapter explores the supply and range of jobs in the future, as well as why changes in the U.S. job distribution have taken place. As much of the explanation for the shift in job distribution over the past several decades is due to the computerization of the workforce, the authors discuss how computers will affect the future composition of the workforce. The chapter also addresses the consequences of educational improvement on earnings distribution. The authors

NEW DIRECTIONS FOR YOUTH DEVELOPMENT • DOI: 10.1002/yd

conclude that beyond workforce preparedness, students need to learn how to be contributing members of a democracy.

Chapter Six: Establishing the R&D agenda for twenty-first century learning

Ken Kay, Margaret Honey

An infusion of twenty-first century skills into American public education necessitates a plan for research and development to further such reform. While the nation agrees that students must obtain critical thinking, problem-solving, and communication skills to succeed in the current global marketplace, this chapter puts forth a long-term, proactive agenda to invest in targeted research to propel and sustain this shift in education. The authors examine the impact such an R&D agenda would have on pedagogy and assessment and the implications for institutions of higher education.

As the United States struggles to maintain dominance in the international economy, it faces a great challenge in keeping up with European and Asian competitors' strategies for preparing youth for the global marketplace. The authors hope the global reality will help contextualize the debate around American education—the current trend toward basics and accountability needs to be broadened. Building on frameworks created by the Partnership for 21st Century Skills, this chapter proposes questions to guide research around teaching, professional development, and assessment significant to twenty-first century skills. Knowing that educational change depends on providing teachers with the tools, support, and training to make fundamental changes in their practice, the authors argue for extensive research around best practices. In addition, if assessments are created to measure the desired outcomes, such measuring tools can drive reform. Furthermore, large-scale changes in teacher preparation programs must take place to allow teachers to adequately employ twenty-first century teaching and assessment strategies.

Chapter Seven: Twenty-first century learning in afterschool

Eric Schwarz, David Stolow

Twenty-first century skills increasingly represent the ticket to the middle class. Yet, the authors argue, in-school learning is simply not enough to help students develop these skills. The authors make the case that after-school (or out-of-school) learning programs are emerging as one of the nation's most promising strategies for preparing young people for the workforce and civic life.

Most school systems have significant limitations for teaching twenty-first century skills. They have the limits of time: with only six hours per day there is barely enough time to teach even the basic skills, especially for those students starting already behind. They have the limits of structure: typical school buildings and classrooms are not physically set up for innovative learning. They have the limits of inertia and bureaucracy: school systems are notoriously resistant to change. And perhaps most important, they have the limits of priorities: especially with the onset of the No Child Left Behind Act, schools are laserlike in their focus on teaching the basics and therefore have less incentive to incorporate twenty-first century skills.

Meanwhile, the authors argue that after-school programs are an untapped resource with three competitive advantages. First, they enable students to work collaboratively in small groups, a setup on which the modern economy will increasingly rely. Second, they are well suited to project-based learning and the development of mastery. Third, they allow students to learn in the real-world contexts that make sense.

Yet the after-school sector is fraught with challenges. It lacks focus—Is it child care, public safety, homework tutoring? And it lacks rigorous results. The authors argue that the teaching of twenty-first century skills should become the new organizing principle for afterschool that will propel the field forward and more effectively bridge in-school and out-of-school learning.

Chapter Eight: Twenty-first century learning in schools: A case study of New Technology High School in Napa, California

Bob Pearlman

The most pertinent question concerning teaching and learning in the twenty-first century is not *what* knowledge and skills students need—that laundry list was identified over a decade ago—but rather *how* to foster twenty-first century learning. What curricula, experiences, assessments, environments, and technology best support twenty-first century learning? New Technology High School (NTHS) in Napa, California, is one example of a successful twenty-first century school. In this chapter, the author describes the components of this exemplary high school, illustrating an environment that will cultivate twenty-first century student learning.

New Technology High School began by defining eight learning outcomes, aligned with the standards of the Partnership for 21st Century Skills; to graduate, students demonstrate mastery of these outcomes through an online portfolio. To help students achieve the outcomes, NTHS employs project- and problem-based learning. Whereas in traditional classrooms students work alone on short-term assignments that do not lend themselves to deep understanding, the project-based learning approach has students working in teams on long-term, in-depth, rigorous projects. Students' work is supported by the school's workplace-like environment and effective use of technology. Meaningful assessment is essential to project-based learning; students receive continuous feedback, helping them become self-directed learners. In fact, NTHS uses outcome-based grading through which students constantly know how they are performing on the twenty-first century outcomes.

Research has shown that NTHS graduates are better prepared for postsecondary education, careers, and citizenship than their peers from other schools. To facilitate twenty-first century learning, all schools need to rethink their approach to teaching and learning. New Technology High School is one way to do so.

Chapter Nine: Twenty-first century learning in school systems: The case of the Metropolitan School District of Lawrence Township, Indianapolis, Indiana

Marcia Capuano and Troy Knoderer

To empower students with skills such as information and technological literacy, global awareness and cultural competence, self-direction, and sound reasoning, teachers must master these skills themselves. This chapter examines how the Digital Age Literacy Initiative of the Metropolitan School District of Lawrence Township in Indianapolis, Indiana, which is funded by the Lilly Endowment, incorporated twenty-first century learning through a systemic approach involving teacher training and the use of data.

The authors explain the district's content, process, and context goals toward accomplishing its mission of empowering students with the necessary twenty-first century skills to succeed in the digital age. The district places a strong emphasis on professional development for teachers. To support the necessary teacher learning and therefore sustain the work of the initiative, the district has adopted action research, self-assessment, and an online professional development network. To support teachers in implementing new strategies, master teachers serve as digital age literacy coaches.

The chapter discusses the initiative's focus on evidence of progress. Through a partnership with the Metiri Group of California, the district has built a range of assessments including online inventories and twenty-first century skill rubrics. For example, the Mankato Survey collected teacher and student data around access, ability, and use of technology in the classroom in 2001 and then in 2004. This research showed significant gains in some technologies across all grade levels and consistent gains in nearly all technologies for middle and high school students.

As it moves into the next phase of implementing the Digital Age Literacy Initiative, the district embraces the systemic shifts in school culture necessary to institutionalize twenty-first century learning.

Chapter Ten: Twenty-first century learning in states: The case of the Massachusetts educational system

David P. Driscoll

A current crisis in education is leaving students less prepared to succeed in the working world than any generation before them. Increasingly complex external, nonacademic pressures have an impact on many of today's students, often causing them to drop out of school. Only 76 percent of Massachusetts high school students graduate, and only 29 percent earn a college degree. National figures are worse.

Most educational institutions share a common goal to support students in becoming skilled, productive, successful members of society, but the author argues that this goal is not being met. Despite the constant changes in the world, educational practices have remained static. Most public schools are not adapting to meet the shifting needs of students. Universities are not able to prepare the right mix of prospective employees for the demands of the job market; for example, schools are graduating only 10 percent of the needed engineers. Institutions of higher learning cannot keep up with employers' needs in an evolving global market: strong math, science,

NEW DIRECTIONS FOR YOUTH DEVELOPMENT • DOI: 10.1002/yd

and writing abilities; critical thinking skills; and the ability to work in teams.

The author draws on exemplary efforts at work in his home state of Massachusetts—whose improvements in student achievement outcomes have been some of the best in the nation—to suggest there is promise in twenty-first century learning. Middle school students involved in a NASA-funded project write proposals, work in teams, and engage in peer review. Older students participate in enhanced, hands-on cooperative school-to-work and after-school programs. Schools are starting to offer expanded day learning, increasing the number of hours they are engaged in formal learning. Yet such programs have not reached significant levels of scale. The author calls for a major shift in education to help today's students be successful in the twenty-first century.

Chapter Eleven: Twenty-first century learning after school: The case of 4-H

Cathann Kress

Founded in the early 1900s, the 4-H Youth Development program can serve as a model for out-of-school programs of the twenty-first century. The 4-H pledge, repeated by its members—over 7 million, ranging in age from five to twenty—articulates its core values: "I pledge: My head to clearer thinking, My heart to greater loyalty, My hands to larger service, and My health to better living for my club, my community, my country, and my world."

The 4-H Development movement was created to provide opportunities for rural children, to help them become constructive adults. Through an emphasis on "learning by doing," 4-H teaches children the habits of lifelong learning. Historically, 4-H has tapped into university-level advancements, extending such knowledge to youth and thereby giving them early access to scientific discoveries and technological progress. Members apply this learning in their communities through hands-on projects crossing a wide-range of pertinent topics.

Research shows that 4-H members are more successful in school than other children and develop a wide range of skills essential in the twenty-first century. Thus, the author makes the case that the foundation of 4-H is exceptionally relevant in today's complex world, perhaps even more so than a century ago. 4-H is a leader in youth development, making it a natural model for twenty-first century after-school programs. Expanding on the 4-H pledge, the author outlines the principles a successful youth development program would have: an emphasis on leadership skills, a feeling of connection and belonging, a forum for exploring career opportunities, and a component of meaningful community service.

Chapter Twelve: Twenty-first century learning after school: The case of Junior Achievement Worldwide

John M. Box

Efforts to increase after-school programming indicate the nation's concern about how youth are engaged during out-of-school time. There are clear benefits to extending the learning that goes on during the school day. Research from the U.S. Departments of Education and Justice shows that after-school participants do better in school and have stronger expectations for the future than youth who are not occupied after school. And the need is evident: 14.3 million students return to an empty house after school, yet only 6.5 million children are currently enrolled in after-school programs. If an after-school program were available, parents of 15.3 million would enroll their child.

JA Worldwide began in 1919 and has been rooted in the after-school arena from its origins. Its after-school programs teach students about the free enterprise system through curriculum focusing on business, citizenship, economics, entrepreneurship, ethics and character, financial literacy, and career development. At the same

NEW DIRECTIONS FOR YOUTH DEVELOPMENT • DOI: 10.1002/yd

time, JA Worldwide incorporates hands-on learning and engage-ment with adults as role models, both key elements to a successful after-school program.

Now focused on developing curriculum emphasizing skills needed for the twenty-first century, JA adopted the key elements laid out for after-school programs by the Partnership for 21st Cen-tury Skills. To ensure that the next generation of students enters the workforce prepared, America's education system must provide the required knowledge, skills, and attitudes. Programs such as JA Worldwide serve as models of how to provide the twenty-first cen-tury skills that all students need to succeed.

Chapter Thirteen: Twenty-first century learning for teachers: Helping educators bring new skills into the classroom

John I. Wilson

The motivation behind every educator's dedication and hard work in the classroom is the knowledge that his or her teaching will result in students' success in life. Educators are committed to implementing twenty-first century skills; they have no question that students need such skills to be equipped for life beyond school. Members of the National Education Association are enthusiastic about the Partnership for 21st Century Skills framework, yet express frustration that many schools do not have adequate resources to make the necessary changes. Teaching these skills poses significant new responsibilities for schools and educators. To make it possible for teachers to build twenty-first century skills into the curriculum, physical and policy infrastructures must exist, pro-fessional development and curriculum materials must be offered, and meaningful assessments must be available.

With an established understanding of what skills need to be infused into the classroom—problem solving, analysis, and com-munications—and educators' commitment to the new skill set, this chapter explores how to make such a dramatic reform happen. The author discusses existing strategies that will guide educators in infusing twenty-first century skills into traditional content areas such as math, English, geography, and science.

Ultimately, public policy regarding educational standards, professional development, assessments, and physical school structures must exist to enable educators to employ twenty-first century skills, leading to student success in contemporary life. Any concern about the cost of bringing this nation's educational system up to par internationally should be offset by the price that not making twenty-first century skills a priority in the classroom will have on future economic well-being.

Chapter Fourteen: Twenty-first century skills for students: Hands-on learning after school builds school and life success

Leide Cabral

At the core of the movement for twenty-first century skills are students. The growing efforts to increase programs leveraging out-of-school time are focused on giving American youth everything they need to compete in this increasingly complex world.

The author is one of many students who have been well served by initiatives imparting twenty-first century skills during after-school hours. Now a senior at Boston Latin School, the author has been helped along the way by Citizen Schools, an after-school education program focused on hands-on learning apprenticeships and homework help. While enrolled in the program as a middle school student, the author took part in projects that exemplified hands-on, inquiry-based learning that helped her develop twenty-first century skills. For example, along with dozens of other students, she advanced her data analysis skills by analyzing statistics about Boston Public high schools, which also helped her select and enroll in one of the city's premier exam schools. Also, she and her peers worked with corporate attorneys who served as writing coaches and whose

NEW DIRECTIONS FOR YOUTH DEVELOPMENT • DOI: 10.1002/yd

expertise the author drew from in producing a published essay and greatly improving her writing skills.

The author now finds that the public speaking, leadership, organizational, social, and management abilities she built through her participation in Citizen Schools are a great asset to her in high school. The confidence with which she tackles her responsibilities can also be traced back to her experiences in the program. As she looks toward college, the author reflects and realizes that being actively involved in a quality after-school program put her on track for a successful future.

As a major American employer and a company at the forefront of technology, Dell recognizes the demands of the modern workforce and promotes twenty-first-century learning in schools.

1

Why American business demands twenty-first century skills: An industry perspective

Karen Bruett

Foreword

A solid global strategy must be part of every organization's DNA. For Dell, this means expanding into new countries where we can use our direct model to provide value to customers and create more productive, healthier communities. It also means hiring employees who think and act globally and have a commitment to learn how to work with cultures other than their own.

It is critical that the United States prepare our students to be competitive in the global economy, an economy that would not be possible without modern technology. For our students to thrive and make meaningful contributions, they will need a command of twenty-first century skills such as self-direction, problem solving, communication and collaboration, and technology proficiency.

NEW DIRECTIONS FOR YOUTH DEVELOPMENT, NO. 110, SUMMER 2006 © WILEY PERIODICALS, INC.
Published online in Wiley InterScience (www.interscience.wiley.com) • DOI: 10.1002/yd.163

As a leading provider of technology to the education community, Dell is committed to providing students with access to relevant technology to enrich their learning experience and introduce them to the world beyond their classroom and communities. Through our work with students and schools, we have seen that technology provides students with more than just technology know-how. It engages them and gives them the confidence to pursue their dreams—and provides them with a very good chance of reaching their goals.

Michael Dell

HOW CAN WE BEST prepare students to succeed in the twenty-first century? This is a question that should resonate with America's educators, employers, parents, policymakers, and the public. Prosperity is based on personal quality of life, community vibrancy, business competitiveness, and economic viability. These all depend on a well-prepared, informed citizenry and workforce.

Public education is the bedrock from which our national and individual prosperity rises. And as a nation, we would be remiss not to ask how we are faring. The truth is that our students fare poorly on national assessments and international comparisons of academic performance. The most recent National Assessment of Educational Progress[1] and the Trends in International Mathematics and Science Study[2] have shown lackluster gains or no gains at all in student achievement for many basic skill areas. Clearly, we have made some progress, but without dramatic change, many young Americans will struggle to thrive in an increasingly competitive global economy.

Changing education

Competitiveness for both businesses and individuals comes down to skills and how they are developed, maintained, strengthened, and applied. Success is defined not only by what someone knows, but how he or she applies that knowledge. The workplace of today and

NEW DIRECTIONS FOR YOUTH DEVELOPMENT • DOI: 10.1002/yd

tomorrow demands and will continue to demand new and different competencies. Work is fundamentally being redefined. It has become more autonomous. Employees at all levels need the ability to solve problems and use complex information to make decisions. No one truly works alone. Teams are global or virtual in nature, and collaboration is expected. In addition, everyone, regardless of occupation, must be able to understand, use, and apply technology to be efficient and effective at work.

Despite these new expectations, a profound gap remains between what students learn in school and what they will need to know when they graduate. We must be vigilant to make education rigorous, meaningful, and relevant to a twenty-first century citizenry and workforce.

Today's students need to know how to apply their knowledge in a real-world environment by thinking critically, analyzing information, comprehending new ideas, communicating, collaborating in teams, and solving problems—all in the context of modern life. We call these competencies *twenty-first century skills.*

There is a growing effort under way to define what twenty-first century learning should look like in our classrooms. Three years ago, the Partnership for 21st Century Skills, of which Dell is a member, set out to identify the skills students need in order to succeed as citizens and workers in the global economy. The organization listened to teachers, students, business leaders, community groups, university faculty, researchers, policymakers, and representatives from underserved communities and then used what they learned to build a framework for building these twenty-first century skills:

- Rigorous core subjects
- Analytical thinking, problem solving, communication, collaboration, and other skills
- Information and communications technology literacy—the ability to use technology tools to acquire learning skills
- Global awareness, civic engagement, and business, financial, and economic literacy
- Measurement of twenty-first century skills

NEW DIRECTIONS FOR YOUTH DEVELOPMENT • DOI: 10.1002/yd

The vision is clear: we must improve student achievement through learning environments aligned to today and the future. In order to accomplish this goal, the partnership is working with education leaders on a state-by-state basis to promote twenty-first century skills in statewide standards and pedagogy, create professional development for teachers that supports advanced learning environments, and bring assessment of twenty-first century skills to education.

As a leading provider of technology to the education community, Dell works with schools to implement technology solutions and programs that help meet their education goals. Specifically, we focus on helping schools:

- Improve student achievement and build twenty-first century skills that will help students succeed in a competitive, global environment
- Increase teacher productivity and meaningful instruction
- Increase administrative effectiveness through data-driven decision making
- Provide opportunity for communities to participate in education

Dell and others are involved in efforts nationwide to measure the impact of new technology-infused models of teaching and learning. Here are a few examples.

- In the 2000–2001 school year, Henrico County Public Schools in Virginia began providing its more than twenty-seven thousand high school and middle school students and teachers with notebook computers, along with professional development in technology for teachers and administrators. The district recently equipped its classrooms with computers, projectors, wireless networks, and other technology devices to make learning more interesting and relevant. Over the next several years, Interactive, an education research firm, will oversee a comprehensive study to determine the impact of technology on student learning, teacher planning and instruction, staff development, and improvement in standardized tests.

- The Texas Education Agency (TEA) took a leadership role in education technology when it launched the Technology Immersion Project (TIP) in 2004. Technology immersion involves providing every teacher and every student at an implementing campus with six key resources: (1) a wireless mobile computing device, (2) productivity software, (3) online content in the core curriculum areas (math, science, social studies, English language arts), (4) online formative assessment tools, (5) ongoing professional development, and (6) on-demand technical support. The project pioneers the concept of total immersion of faculty and students in technology at more than twenty school districts in Texas. Each participating school has been provided with a wireless mobile computing device for every student and teacher, productivity software, online content in the core curriculum areas, online assessment tools, professional development, and technical support. To measure how effective this immersion model is in increasing student achievement in English, math, science, and social studies, the TEA is studying the TIP campuses against control campuses for at least three years. The research aims to determine TIP's immediate and long-term effect on student outcomes, including technology proficiency, performance on standardized achievement tests, student attendance, and dropout rates.

We all can play a role in preparing students to compete in the global economy. Educators and administrators need to advocate for the infusion of twenty-first century skills into education curricula. Legislators can create policies endorsing professional development for teachers and establish state standards and assessments that include these skill requirements. Parents must engage in an ongoing dialogue with educators, administrators, and school board officials to ensure that students are using problem-solving skills, working in teams, and integrating technology into their studies. And employers have an opportunity to partner with local schools to provide students with authentic learning opportunities.

Now is the time to act so that our children can realize their potential as the citizens, workers, and leaders of tomorrow. Students who have developed twenty-first century skills will be ready for whatever the world has in store for them.

Notes

1. Perie, M., Moran, R., & Lutkus, A. D. (2005). *NAEP 2004 trends in academic progress: Three decades of student performance in reading and mathematics.* Washington, DC: National Center for Education Statistics.

2. Gonzales, P., Carlos Guzman, J., Partelow, L., Pahlke, E., Jocelyn, L., Kastberg, D., & Williams, T. (2005). *Highlights from the Trends in International Mathematics and Science Study: TIMSS 2003.* Washington, DC: National Center for Education Statistics.

MICHAEL DELL *is chairman of the board of directors of Dell.*

KAREN BRUETT *is area vice president for Dell's K–12 business and immediate past chair for the Partnership for 21st Century Skills, the leading advocacy organization focused on infusing twenty-first century skills into education.*

Microsoft, one of the world's largest corporations, evaluates its employees' performance against twenty-first century skills and works to improve education in the digital age.

2

Why American business demands twenty-first century learning: A company perspective

Allyson Knox

TODAY'S KNOWLEDGE ECONOMY requires that the citizenry and workforce be able to harness information and communication technologies in order to remain competitive on a global scale. It may come as a surprise to learn that the United States is struggling in this new economic environment:

- Only 13 percent of American adults are proficient in the knowledge and skills needed to search for, comprehend, and use information—a 13 percent drop since 1992.
- Just 13 percent of American adults surveyed are proficient in the knowledge and skills needed to identify and perform computational tasks, a number that has not improved in fifteen years.
- Only 5 percent of American college undergraduates today are pursuing degrees in science or engineering, compared with 42 percent of university students in China.[1]

NEW DIRECTIONS FOR YOUTH DEVELOPMENT, NO. 110, SUMMER 2006 © WILEY PERIODICALS, INC.
Published online in Wiley InterScience (www.interscience.wiley.com) • DOI: 10.1002/yd.164

As a result of new demands, the notion of digital literacy has become less a luxury and more an imperative for many countries, gaining significant momentum in the past decade among government officials, business leaders, and educators. In particular, technology companies, many of which have led the charge into the digital age, have been instrumental in designing tools we use every day and in teaching us how to use and benefit from those tools.

Many technology companies work with schools and communities through corporate giving or volunteer initiatives to facilitate technology skills training to prepare students for careers in the digital age. But although students and parents are often told that computer skills are integral to their education, often it can be difficult for them to envision how those skills will be used in their future careers. What exactly are the current and future demands that employees face? What does it take to work in this new information-based economy, and what might such a job look like?

Although perhaps unique in its size and position, Microsoft's corporate culture is indicative of the kinds of job skills that are now critical for success. Much in the way that the company invests in education and workforce development to prepare citizens to learn and work in the global economy, Microsoft also holds its employees accountable to a set of core competencies that enables the company to remain competitive and innovative.

These competencies have evolved since the company's inception and continue to change and grow as the economy demands new skills, products, and services. Microsoft's competencies and the Partnership for 21st Century Skills learning framework both feature a consistent package of abilities to ensure individuals are competitive in the future and beyond. The Partnership for 21st Century Skills learning framework emphasizes core subjects as well as twenty-first century learning skills, tools, content, context, and assessments. Microsoft core competencies emphasize capabilities such as intellectual strength, self-development, cross-collaboration skills, and interpersonal skills. At Microsoft, competencies are used for a variety of purposes, ranging from

NEW DIRECTIONS FOR YOUTH DEVELOPMENT • DOI: 10.1002/yd

job descriptions and shaping job interview questions on a more basic level, to guiding employees' career development plans and managing employee performance. Each competency is broken down into four levels of proficiencies to specify and clarify what they are and what they look like in action.

Parallels between the two sets of competencies are clear. For example, under the "results" competency, Microsoft believes that employees should be able to recognize patterns among systems in order to solve problems as they arise. Within the learning skills area of the Partnership for 21st Century Skills framework, it is recommended that students be able to exercise sound reasoning when making complex choices and understand the interconnections among systems. Accordingly, the company also recognizes a certain degree of uncertainty, given the complexity of such systems, the context of the decision at hand, and the information (or lack thereof) available to the decision maker. Thus, a unique shared competency urges people to accept and even embrace the uncomfortable world of ambiguity. Microsoft advocates that its employees be able to deal with ambiguity and embrace unfamiliar challenges. Similarly, the Partnership for 21st Century Skills states that under "interpersonal and self-directional skills," individuals should be able to "tolerate ambiguity." Both sets of competencies require individuals to use and embrace technology as an essential tool for learning and working while emphasizing the importance of being able to function and contribute as a team player.

It is in the spirit of these core competencies and its general mandate to empower individuals to achieve success in the knowledge economy that Microsoft established the worldwide Partners in Learning (PiL) initiative. PiL is designed to assist individuals and communities in increasing access to the technologies and skills that they need to succeed in the changing economy by building education partnerships with governments, education leaders, and institutions. Within the United States, PiL works to build public-private partnerships that advance teaching, learning, and digital inclusion projects.

One of PiL's projects is a three-year initiative: the Microsoft/ Philadelphia School of the Future Project. The school, which will focus on creating a sustainable and replicable model for improved instruction through the use of technology and systemic reform, will open in the fall of 2006. Twenty-first century leaders became a critical first step in creating a twenty-first century learning environment. Hence, the district modeled the needed competencies after Microsoft's Career Development Competencies and the Partnership for 21st Century Skills framework (see Figure 2.1). These competencies, called the "Education Competencies," represent many of the attributes, behaviors, knowledge, skills, and abilities required for successful job performance. Competencies include a definition, four levels of proficiency, sample interview questions, developmental activities and resources, and a description of overdoing the competency. "Hiring and developing great people is the key to any organization's success," says Mary Cullinane, PiL program manager. "The HR processes developed and used for the School of the Future set a strong foundation for future success" (personal communication).

The PiL grants designed to discover local and regional twenty-first century learning education innovations are known as the Mid-Tier projects. There are twelve of these projects throughout the nation. The common elements of the twelve projects are to scale or spread the projects on multiple dimensions; use technology throughout the scaling process; learn about the relationships among technology, scaling, and promising practices; and share findings with business and education leaders.

Evidence of twenty-first century learning and teaching is featured in all of the projects—for example:

• Alabama Best Practices Center, a statewide nonprofit organization, works extensively with a cadre of local educational leaders committed to training teachers and administrators on twenty-first century learning.
• Global Kids, a nonprofit organization based in New York City, trains students to design online games focused on global social

NEW DIRECTIONS FOR YOUTH DEVELOPMENT • DOI: 10.1002/yd

Figure 2.1. Building the School of the Future: The Education Competencies.

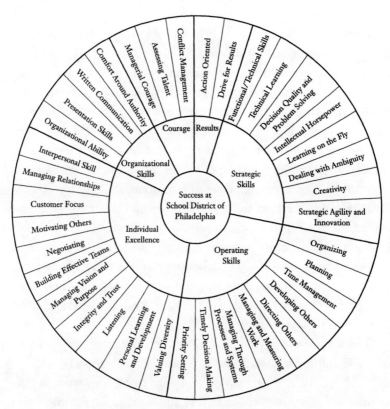

Source: The Education Competencies are available to educators for free at http://www.microsoft.com/education/competencies/default.mspx.

issues, resonating with the Partnership for 21st Century Skills' civic and global competencies.

• Council of Independent Colleges, a national association based in Washington, D.C., is working with member colleges as they rework teacher education curricula to emphasize twenty-first century teaching and learning strategies.

• The National Commission on Teaching and America's Future is building a virtual professional learning community designed to support novice teachers. This project explores whether strategies such as online mentoring or targeted online resources improve novice teacher retention rates.

Another key component of PiL is establishing five-year public-private partnerships with six states (Florida, Michigan, New Mexico, Pennsylvania, Virginia, and Washington) to provide investment funding for innovative solutions that have yet to be developed or deployed. The goal is to support a broad and diverse set of long-term strategic twenty-first century learning models that can serve as blueprints for other schools or educators across the United States. For example, the State of Washington, Microsoft, Eastern Washington University's College of Education, and Cheney School District will join efforts to help preservice and in-service teachers learn how to tailor their classroom instruction to meet students' individual needs in reading, writing, and math. The end product will be a professional K–20 collaborative culture that leads to continuous improvement. As another example, New Mexico and Microsoft will work together to align the states' education and economic development strategies.

Over a five-year period, Microsoft's PiL initiative will donate over $35 million to assist state and local governments and education communities to develop partnerships that advance the use of technology to improve education. In addition, public schools, universities, and others will have the opportunity to leverage the expertise of one of the world's most innovative companies to help with their own efforts through direct contact with Microsoft employees. Thus, while each project uniquely addresses a variety of the challenges in education today, they demonstrate that Microsoft not only advocates for twenty-first century skills but uses them in making and strengthening educational partners.

The challenges of competing in the innovation economy and teaching today's students are substantial but not insurmountable. The investments made through Partners in Learning are creating a multitude of resources—leadership training, teacher development, curriculum and assessments tools, and school-based technology support—that can help others establish sustainable models for digital inclusion and twenty-first century teaching and learning.

Notes

1. Passman, P. (2006). "Preparing American Workers for the Knowledge Economy: A Call to Action." Speech delivered at National Association of Workforce Boards Forum 2006, Washington, D.C., Feb. 27, 2006. Retrieved Mar. 6, 2006, from http://www.microsoft.com/presspass/exec/passman/02-27-06Workforce.mspx.

ALLYSON KNOX *is academic program manager for United States Partners in Learning at Microsoft, a global initiative of the company to provide funding, equipment, and content to promote twenty-first century learning and teaching and digital inclusion.*

Results from a national opinion survey show broad support for twenty-first century learning in the form of "basics-plus" education.

3

Why the American public supports twenty-first century learning

Michele Sacconaghi

A KEY COMPONENT IN making the case for twenty-first century learning is building a broad foundation of support for it among important constituent groups. How knowledgeable is the public at large about twenty-first century skills? How receptive are people to a more concerted effort to incorporate twenty-first century learning in school and in after-school programs?

American attitudes toward the need for teaching twenty-first century skills appear as strong as the socioeconomic research being done that shows how critical these skills are for students' future access to the middle class and the country's economic competitiveness. In 2003, the AOL Time Warner Foundation (now the Time Warner Foundation) set out to measure public attitudes toward twenty-first century skills. It commissioned national research firms Lake, Snell, Perry and Associates and Market Strategies to conduct a telephone survey with 1,000 adults, including 100 African Americans, 100 Latinos, 150 teachers, and 150 business executives. In June 2003, the findings from the survey were published in *Twenty-First Century Literacy: A Vital Component in Learning*.[1]

NEW DIRECTIONS FOR YOUTH DEVELOPMENT, NO. 110, SUMMER 2006 © WILEY PERIODICALS, INC.
Published online in Wiley InterScience (www.interscience.wiley.com) • DOI: 10.1002/yd.165

The survey shows that Americans believe that students today need a "basics-plus" education: not only competency in the basics of reading, writing, and mathematics but also a package of skills different from those needed ten to twenty years ago to succeed in school and in life. The survey also showed that Americans view after-school programming as a vehicle for teaching and learning these skills.

Figures 3.1 to 3.5 provide detail on some of the findings. Here are a few highlights from the national opinion survey:

- Ninety-two percent of respondents think that young people need different skills today than they did ten to twenty years ago.
- Ninety-one percent said it is "very" or "somewhat" important to "prepare young people with twenty-first century literacy skills."
- Ninety percent think this is an important issue, even "given the current challenges that face the education system."

Figure 3.1. Attitudes on necessary skills

Do you think youth and teens today, to be successful in life, need to learn very different skills from what were needed ten to twenty years ago, somewhat different skills, or not that different skills? (Split sampled—asked of only half of respondents.)

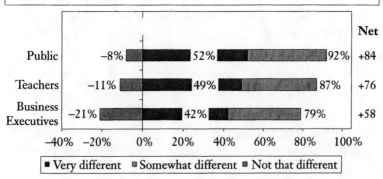

Source: Time Warner Foundation. (2003, June). *Twenty-first century literacy: A vital component in learning.* Survey conducted by Lake Snell Perry & Associates and Market Strategies. New York: Time Warner Foundation.

Figure 3.2. Attitudes on how well prepared American youth are

Thinking about skills for life and work in the twenty-first century, do you think American youth are behind, ahead, or about as well prepared as youth in other advanced industrialized countries?

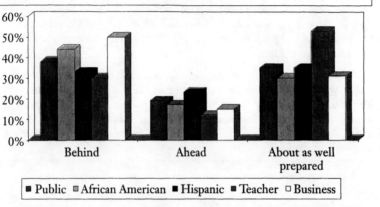

Source: Time Warner Foundation. (2003, June). *Twenty-first century literacy: A vital component in learning.* Survey conducted by Lake Snell Perry & Associates and Market Strategies. New York: Time Warner Foundation.

- Seventy percent favor a basics-plus education over a back-to-basics approach for young people.
- While almost 70 percent of Americans generally believe schools are preparing young people for life after graduation, only 19 percent think they are being prepared "very well."
- Seventy-four percent think teens are learning basic skills, and 60 percent think they are being taught to use technology effectively. However, only 48 percent believe teens are learning communication skills, only 37 percent think they are getting critical thinking and decision-making skills, and only 28 percent believe young people are learning how to make a difference in their community.
- Only 42 percent think schools are doing a good job teaching young people the twenty-first century literacy skills they need.

Figure 3.3. Attitudes on approaches to education

Next, I am going to read two statements people have made about education. Please tell me which one comes closer to your own point of view.

Back to Basics: [Some/other] people say the basics of reading, writing,
and math are the foundation for a good education. By mastering these
core skills, young people can succeed in school and later in life. A back-
to-basics philosophy is the best approach for producing lifelong learners
and a strong workforce.

Basics Plus: [Some/other] people say that the basics of reading, writing,
and math alone are no longer enough to succeed in school and later on in
life. In the twenty-first century, young people need to learn a broad range
of skills like new technologies, critical thinking, and communication. A
basics plus philosophy is the best approach for producing lifelong learners
and a strong workforce.

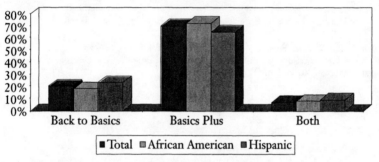

Note: Even the groups most oriented toward the basics, such as seniors, those who live
in suburban areas, and Republican men, support the basics-plus approach two-to-one.

Source: Time Warner Foundation. (2003, June). *Twenty-first century literacy: A vital component in learning.* Survey conducted by Lake Snell Perry & Associates and Market
Strategies. New York: Time Warner Foundation.

- Eighty-nine percent agree that there "should be some type of
  organized activity or place for children and teens to go after
  school that provides opportunities for them to learn."
- Fifty-nine percent felt that "access to high quality after-school
  and summer programs that include these skills" would be effective in getting skills to young people.

We believe that this survey shows there is ample opportunity to
establish broad-based support for twenty-first century learning. In

Figure 3.4. Attitudes on important skills that youth will need

Now let me read to you different skills that youth and teens may need in the twenty-first century. For each skill, please tell me how important it is for them to have in the twenty-first century—one of the most important, very important, somewhat important, a little important, or not important at all. (Split sampled.)

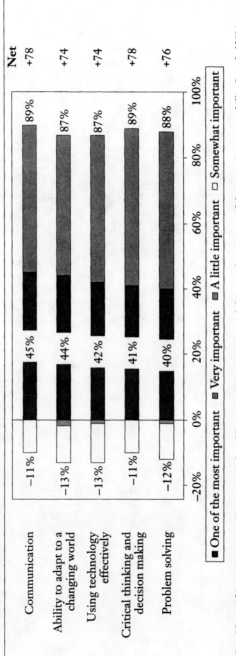

Note: More African Americans (51 percent) than Hispanics (39 percent) see ability to adapt as one of the most important skills. Over half (54 percent) of business executives see using technology effectively as one of the most important skills. Critical thinking and decision making are among the most important for more than half of teachers (56 percent). Teachers (51 percent) and business executives (44 percent) are also intense on problem solving.

Source: Time Warner Foundation. (2003, June). *Twenty-first century literacy: A vital component in learning.* Survey conducted by Lake Snell Perry & Associates and Market Strategies. New York: Time Warner Foundation.

Figure 3.5. Attitudes on less strongly needed skills for youth

Now let me read to you different skills that youth and teens may need in the twenty-first century. For each one please tell me how important a skill it is for youth to have in the twenty-first century—one of the most important, very important, somewhat important, a little important, or not important at all. (Split sampled.)

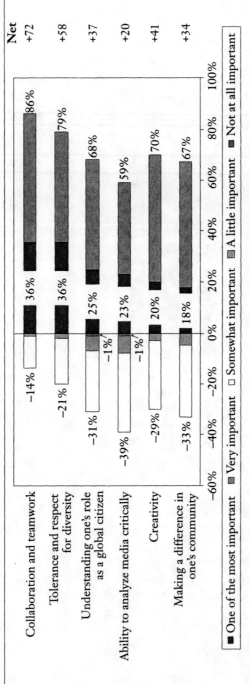

Note: African Americans and Hispanics are more intense on tolerance and respect for diversity (46 and 42 percent, respectively). Only a quarter of Hispanics see collaboration and teamwork as among the most important skills (25 percent).

Source: Time Warner Foundation. (2003, June). *Twenty-first century literacy: A vital component in learning.* New York: Time Warner Foundation. Survey conducted by Lake Snell Perry & Associates and Market Strategies. New York: Time Warner Foundation.

the words of Ken Kay, president of the Partnership for 21st Century Skills, the survey "will help build momentum for an improved model of education for the new millennium."

Note

1. Time Warner Foundation. (2003, June). *Twenty-first century literacy: A vital component in learning.* Survey conducted by Lake Snell Perry & Associates and Market Strategies. New York: Time Warner Foundation.

MICHELE SACCONAGHI *is executive director of the Time Warner Foundation, which provides funding for after-school, college access, leadership development, and media and technology programs for youth.*

The nation's achievement gap must be examined within the context of the increasing economic demand for higher-level skills.

4

Why America's disadvantaged communities need twenty-first century learning

Blenda J. Wilson

IN MOST CONTEMPORARY discussions about the achievement gap—between rich and poor students, and between Asian and white students on the one hand, and African American and Hispanic students on the other—the underlying assumption is that educational reform can eliminate it. Educational reform efforts, focused on testing and data-driven accountability, including the underlying principles of No Child Left Behind, have certainly enabled us to understand the pervasiveness and dimensions of educational inequality. Requirements to disaggregate scores by income, race, and ethnicity now enable us to document the correlation between academic attainment and income.

Research indicates that the achievement gap begins before kindergarten.[1] Disadvantaged children have less access to books and libraries than children growing up in more economically

Thanks to Laura Su and Philippa Mulford for their research assistance.

advantaged families. Poor children, particularly minorities, do not enter school with the same level of language mastery or social and communication skills as their middle-class peers. Because lower-income parents often feel alienated from the school culture, they may not be as effective in advocating for quality education for their children. From the earliest years of schooling on, disadvantaged students continue to fall behind, in part because they lack access to the enriching environments that children in middle- and upper-class communities do.[2]

The consequences of these differences are revealed in the gap in educational and economic attainment of poor students. Low-income students are six times more likely to drop out of high school than upper-income students.[3] Moreover, half of the heads of households on welfare and half of the prison population are headed by high school dropouts.[4] These patterns of inequity are exacerbated when applied to populations that are both poor and African American or Hispanic.

It is important to place the discussion of the achievement gap within the larger context of the increasing demand for higher levels of learning for everyone. Wages for high school dropouts and high school graduates with no college have declined over the past generation, while wages for the most educated workers are rising sharply. We can document the increasing economic premium of a college education versus just a high school education. In 2003, the average full-time year-round worker with a four-year college degree earned $49,000—62 percent more than the $30,800 earned by the average full-time worker with only a high school diploma.[5] For blue-collar workers, maintaining a middle-class standard of living requires two breadwinners to support a family.[6]

When we talk about the achievement gap without taking into account the dramatic change in society's needs and expectations for education, we tend to ignore the fact that schools are not only failing to educate disadvantaged students but are also failing to educate all students to the level of international excellence to which our country aspires.

NEW DIRECTIONS FOR YOUTH DEVELOPMENT • DOI: 10.1002/yd

Researchers Richard Murnane and Frank Levy, in Chapter Five in this volume and in their previous work, highlight the necessity of more fundamental changes in our education systems by defining the new basic skills essential in the twenty-first century technology-based economy. These skills include the ability to solve new problems that cannot be solved by a set of rules; the ability to transmit, interpret, and communicate information to others; reading and mathematics competency at the ninth-grade level; and the ability to form and test a hypothesis in order to solve semistructured problems. In addition, the workforce demands employees who can work well in diverse groups, communicate effectively orally and in writing, and use computers for a wide range of basic tasks.[7]

What is most damning about Levy and Murnane's research is their estimate that as many as half of U.S. students who do graduate from high school enter the workforce lacking the skills necessary to succeed. What happens to young people who do not graduate from high school or graduate but fail to master both the traditional skills taught in high school and the new skills required in today's workplaces? They are relegated to service sector jobs that do not pay enough to support families.

The logical conclusion is that our country is producing a generation of citizens who may not make it into the middle class.[8]

America's disadvantaged communities need twenty-first century learning because all children need to be better educated. Moreover, some of what we have learned by seeking improvements in learning for disadvantaged students can provide models for engagement in learning and development of new skills that will better serve all populations.

A growing movement in support of academically and socially enriched out-of-school-time programs is providing powerful evidence that society can overcome gaps in opportunity that lead to gaps in achievement. The movement has been spurred in part by changes in the structure of families: Americans are working more hours and have less vacation time than workers in other industrialized countries, and almost 74 percent of employed women with children under eighteen worked full-time.[9]

Another factor is related to the new imperative for all children to meet the requirements of standards based educational reform. This has forced educators to acknowledge that children are in school only 20 percent of their time—180 days per year for six or seven hours a day. The remaining 80 percent of their time reveals wide and significant differences in the experiences of poor and advantaged children—what we call the opportunity gap—sufficient to explain some, if not all, of the deficiencies in academic preparedness and achievement of low-income and minority children.

Middle- and upper-class children have ready access to a wide variety of enrichment activities. Those growing up in low-income communities, urban and rural, are far less likely to have access to such activities, particularly if they take place outside school.[10]

The good news is that research shows that quality after-school programs play an important and effective role in giving all children access to experiences, mentors, and the skills they need to contribute in today's economy, to graduate from high school, and to go on to postsecondary education. In addition to helping students take advantage of networks and community-based learning resources like museums and libraries, after-school programs help to ensure that all children are exposed to enrichment activities and opportunities to practice essential communication, thinking, and teamwork skills.

Critical Hours: Afterschool Programs and Educational Success documents the correlation between effective after-school programs and academic success. Research studies indicate:[11]

• Compared to students who spent five to nineteen hours per week in school-sponsored extracurricular activities, students who had not were six times more likely to have dropped out by senior year, three times more likely to have been suspended in sophomore or senior year, and twice as likely to have been arrested by senior year.

• A longitudinal study that began in seventh grade found that among at-risk students, the dropout rate was markedly lower for those who had participated in extracurricular activities compared with those who had not.

- Middle school students who spend three or more hours home alone after school are significantly more likely to use drugs and alcohol, have high levels of stress and anger, experience more depression and behavior problems, possess lower self-esteem, and perform less well academically.
- Students who participate in extracurricular activities and community service typically have higher academic achievement; behave better in school; and have better work habits, higher educational aspirations, better relationships with parents, and a greater sense of belonging in the community.

Many after-school programs have been designed specifically to support improved academic outcomes for disadvantaged students. Those that provide help with homework and access to computers, in addition to the general benefits described above, also reduce educational inequity, particularly for students who do not have computers at home or parents who speak English.

Effective after-school programs are not just "more school." On the contrary, the best programs increase students' engagement in learning; offer a variety of active, experiential activities students themselves choose to participate in; strengthen students' relationships with supportive adults; and provide the time necessary for students to master traditional academic skills as well as complex new skills. Reginald Clark, a prominent education researcher, has stated unequivocally, "We can accurately predict a youngster's success or failure in school by finding out whether or not he or she typically spends approximately 20 to 35 hours a week . . . engaging in constructive learning activity."[12]

America's international competitiveness and economic leadership is threatened by an educational system that fails to educate its young people to international levels of excellence. At the same time, the majority of the nation's future youth will come from low-income, immigrant, and minority populations. Schools cannot do it alone. Quality after-school programs can contribute to improving overall educational attainment and eliminating the achievement gap, helping young people develop skills for success.

Notes

1. Lee, V. E., & Burkam, D. T. (2002). *Inequality at the starting gate.* Washington, DC: Economic Policy Institute.

2. Miller, B. M. (2003). *Critical hours: Afterschool programs and educational success.* Quincy, MA: Nellie Mae Education Foundation.

3. Schwarz, E. (2004, November 10). Address to the Institute of Museum and Library Services, Washington, DC.

4. Citizen Schools. (2005, February 28). *Mobilizing a community's citizens for high school success: Citizen Schools and the integration of in-school and out-of-school learning.* Presented at Citizen Schools' Executive briefing to funders.

5. Baum, S., & Payea, K. (2004). *Education pays: The benefits of higher education for individuals and society.* Princeton, NJ: College Board.

6. Schwarz, E. (2005, February). *Realizing the American dream: Historical scorecard, current challenges, future opportunities.* Working paper developed for A Gathering of Leaders: Social Entrepreneurs and Scale in the Twenty-First Century, Mohonk, New York.

7. Murnane, R., & Levy, F. (2004, April 29). *Preparing students to thrive in Twenty First century America: The role for after-school.* Presentation to Reimagining After-School: A Symposium on Learning and Leading in the Twenty First Century, Cambridge, MA.

8. Murnane & Levy. (2004).

9. Loupe, D., and Morrison, A. (2006, May 7). Fair play: If mom got a salary, what would it be? (And don't skimp on overtime). *Sunday Paper.*

10. Miller. (2003).

11. Miller. (2003).

12. Clark, R. M. (1998). *Critical factors in why disadvantaged children succeed or fail in school.* New York: Academy for Educational Development.

BLENDA J. WILSON *is president and CEO of Nellie Mae Education Foundation, New England's largest public charity dedicated exclusively to improving academic achievement for the region's underserved communities.*

A host of data on the makeup of the twenty-first century workforce suggests that educators focus on a new level of skills, including expert thinking and complex communication.

5

Why the changing American economy calls for twenty-first century learning: Answers to educators' questions

Frank Levy, Richard J. Murnane

AS AMERICAN EDUCATORS struggle to meet the unprecedented challenge of preparing all students to master the skills embodied in state learning standards, some wonder whether their efforts make economic sense. After all, the newspapers are full of reports of jobs being outsourced to lower-wage countries and jobs being done by computers. The U.S. Bureau of Labor Statistics (BLS) predicts that the fastest-growing occupation in the United States will be food preparers and servers—low-skilled, low-wage jobs requiring little education. If more and more work is going to be done by computers

This chapter is adapted from the authors' recent book *The New Division of Labor: How Computers Are Creating the Next Job Market* (Princeton University Press, 2004), which was based on the authors' article "Education and the Changing Job Market," *Educational Leadership*, 2004, *62*(2), 1–4. Original materials are used with permission from the Association for Supervision and Curriculum Development (ASCD), a worldwide community of educators advocating sound policies and sharing best practices to achieve the success of each learner.

or by workers in other countries, do current educational reform initiatives make sense?

The purpose of this chapter is to answer questions that educators, parents, and youth ask about the educational implications of changes in the American economy. The main message is that there will be good jobs for well-educated Americans. Indeed, the great danger is the continuing decline in earnings opportunities for Americans who lack the skills to do the growing number of jobs requiring expert thinking and complex communication.

Will there be enough jobs in the future?

In many ways, the current slow recovery repeats the "jobless recovery" of 1992–1994. Just as was true then, prudent fiscal and monetary policy eventually will return the nation to full employment. However, the mix of jobs will continue to change; the jobs lost to computerization and to other countries are not coming back.

How is the job mix changing?

The nation is experiencing a hollowing out of the occupational structure. In Figure 5.1, the nation's occupations are grouped into seven categories, arrayed from lowest paying on the left to highest paying on the right. The categories of jobs that experienced declining importance between 1969 and 1999 are blue-collar jobs including assembly line work and administrative support jobs such as filing and bookkeeping. The lowest-paid category, service sector jobs, which include janitorial work as well as preparing and serving food, is experiencing moderate growth. However, the higher-paid job categories, technicians, professional occupations, and managers, have experienced the greatest growth.

One of the reasons the changes in the nation's job mix have important implications for education is that the occupations experiencing declines have historically provided jobs to the majority of the nation's high school graduates. Young people who leave high school today with the skills to succeed in postsecondary education and training programs needed to gain access to the growing number of relatively high-wage jobs face a bright future. Those who

Figure 5.1. U.S. Adult occupation distribution, 1969–1999

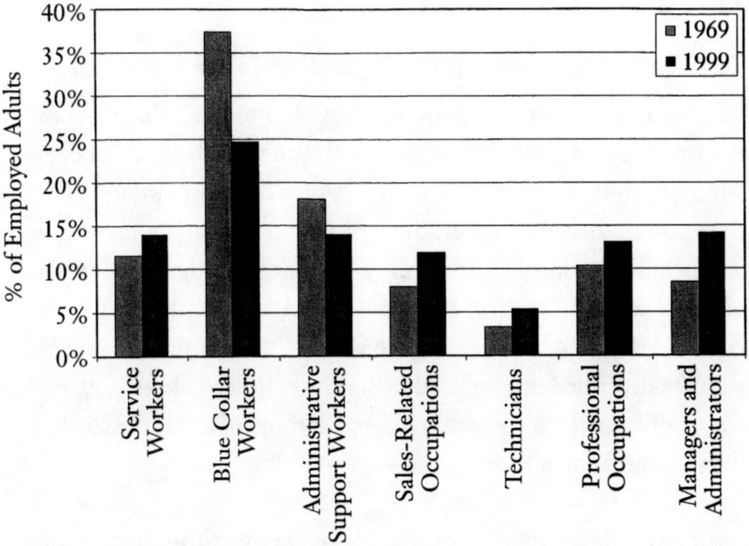

Note: The occupations are listed in order of increasing average salary.

Source: Authors' calculations based on the March 1970 and March 2000 Current Population Surveys conducted by the U.S. Census Bureau.

graduate without the requisite skills will find themselves competing for service sector jobs, the number of which is also growing. Most of these jobs do not pay enough to support families, however, because they are jobs that almost all workers can do.

How can the trends in Figure 5.1 be reconciled with the BLS prediction about food servers and preparers?

In BLS projections, all food service workers fall under one occupational title, and this results in many job openings in a single occupation. In these same projections, a highly skilled category like engineering is divided into multiple specific occupations: aeronautical engineer, mechanical engineer, and so on, each relatively small. In Figure 5.1, specific occupations are combined into broad groups: food service workers grouped with other service workers and aeronautical engineers grouped with other professional occupations.

Looking at these groups, it is clear that job growth is concentrated in higher-skilled occupations.

Why have the changes in the U.S. job distribution taken place?

Advances in computerization are playing a key role in bringing about this change. To understand this process, begin with the fact that every job in the economy requires the processing of information. Words on a page, numbers in a report, the look on a customer's face, the taste of a sauce, the sound of a stumbling automobile engine: people in their daily work process all this information as they decide what to do next. Computers excel at tasks in which the information processing can be described as a series of logical rules (rules-based logic) or in the recognition of simple patterns. An example of a rules-based task is the job of issuing a boarding pass to an airline passenger:

Identify the passenger by reading the account number on her credit card.

Does the number on the credit card match a reservation in the database? (yes/no)

If no—reject the request.

If yes—does the passenger have a seat assignment in the database? (yes/no)

If no—show her the available seats and prompt the customer to choose one.

If yes—complete the transaction.

Because this information can be processed by applying rules, boarding passes increasingly are issued by self-service kiosks rather than by desk agents. The same is true for a great many manufacturing and administrative support jobs. Moreover, when most of a job can be described in rules—that is, codified—it can be moved offshore with minimal risk of misunderstanding. In manufacturing, an example is Boeing's design of aircraft modules using computer-assisted design software (CATIA). CATIA's output is a set of instructions—that is, rules—for computer-controlled machine tools. Some of these machine tools are located in China, Japan, and

Italy because Boeing knows the parts will fit when they are returned for final assembly.

A call center job is codified when everything the operator needs to know can be written in scripts on a computer screen. These are the kinds of jobs that are being sent offshore. Software programming is codified because students everywhere study from the same textbooks and work with the same platforms from Microsoft, Oracle, SAP, and others.

What skills are valued in the computerized workplace?

As illustrated in Figure 5.2, changes in the distribution of the nation's jobs over the period 1969 to 1998 have increased the importance of two types of skills. The first is *expert thinking*, the ability to solve new problems that cannot be solved by applying rules. (If the problem

Figure 5.2. Trends in the tasks done by the American workforce, 1969–1998 (1969 = 0)

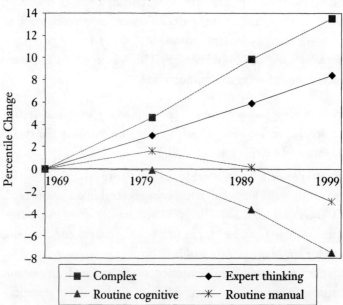

Source: Levy, F., & Murnane, R. J. (2004). *The new division of labor: How computers are creating the next job market.* Princeton, NJ: Princeton University Press.

NEW DIRECTIONS FOR YOUTH DEVELOPMENT • DOI: 10.1002/yd

could be solved by rules, a computer could do it.) New problems run the gamut from doing research, to fixing a new problem in a car that is not covered in the manual, to creating a new dish in a restaurant.

The second type of skill that is growing in importance is *complex communication*, the ability not only to transmit information, but to convey a particular interpretation of information to others in jobs like teaching, selling, and negotiation. If a student gets a calculus lesson from the Web, the student will literally have the information. But there is no guarantee that the student will understand the information she is receiving. It takes a good teacher to present the information in a way that allows the student to translate the information into knowledge she can apply. Complex communication is equally important in sales. Customers who know exactly what they want can order from a Web site without human intervention. But a customer who requires convincing needs subtle human contact. A good salesperson is constantly modifying her argument as she reads the customer's facial expression and listens to the customer's questions and tone of voice. That kind of selling is very hard to express in rules, and so it remains a human endeavor.

Figure 5.2 also illustrates the declining importance of routine manual work such as assembly line work and routine cognitive work such as filing and bookkeeping. The reason is that these are the easiest types of tasks to computerize.

Does the growing importance of expert thinking and complex communication mean that schools should stop teaching the three R's and focus on teaching these skills?

No, for two reasons. First, literacy and math are critical skills necessary to acquire the knowledge to be an expert thinker in any field. Second, the skills needed to be good at complex communication and expert thinking can be taught in any subject area and need not compete for space in the curriculum.

What the changes in the economy make increasingly important is that students learn to use their reading, math, and communication skills to develop and express a deep understanding of the subject matter they are studying. To illustrate, consider the following example, taken from a recent National Research Council report. Two students respond to a short oral quiz:

Student 1

Q: What was the date of battle of the Spanish Armada?
A: 1588.
Q: How do you know this?
A: It was one of the dates I memorized for the exam.
Q: Why is the event important?
A: I don't know.

Student 2

Q: What was the date of battle of the Spanish Armada?
A: It must have been around 1590.
Q: How do you know this?
A: I know the English began to settle in Virginia just after 1600, although I'm not sure of the exact date. They wouldn't have dared start overseas explorations if Spain still had control of the seas. It would have taken a little while to get expeditions organized, so England must have gained naval supremacy somewhere in the late 1500s.
Q: Why is the event important?
A: It marks a turning point in the relative importance of England and Spain as European powers and colonizers of the New World.[1]

Once again, the challenge posed by a changing economy is not to teach new subjects. Instead, it is to teach the subjects currently in the curriculum in a way that enables all students to develop the type of understanding and the communication skills illustrated by the second student's responses.

Aren't computers increasing the range of tasks they can do, creating a real danger of mass unemployment?

The number of tasks computers can do grows every year. If there were a fixed amount of work in the economy, computers' growing capability would translate into mass unemployment. But the amount of work to be done is not fixed. Partly as a result of advances in computerization, new tasks are created each year. For example, computerization made possible complex mutual funds involving derivatives. Valuing these complex new funds is a task that only humans can do because it involves both complex communication and nonroutine problem solving.

We can draw an analogy by going back to 1880, the last year when half of the workforce worked in agriculture. If anyone had predicted then that new machinery would allow all the agriculture we need to be produced by 3 percent of the workforce, people would have assumed that the unemployment rate would soar. The unemployment rate has not soared because people are now doing hundreds of jobs that did not exist in 1880. The way to think about computers (and computer-supported outsourcing) is that they change the economy's mix of jobs, not the number of jobs. In particular, they create new and higher-skill demands for workers.

Are all blue-collar jobs going to disappear?

No. The work of carpenters, plumbers, mechanics, and other craftspeople cannot be done offshore; they have to work at the site of the problem. Moreover, their work cannot be automated because they constantly encounter new problems for which they have to construct new solutions. For example, today's auto repair technicians use computer-based diagnostic tools to test cars' systems. Their real work begins when the computer diagnostics indicate all systems are functioning properly, yet the car is not performing adequately. This illustrates why students preparing for craft jobs in vocational education programs need expert thinking and complex communication skills.

What would be the consequences of educational improvements for the earnings distribution?

If the nation's schools are able to dramatically increase the percentage of students who leave school prepared to succeed in postsecondary education and training programs, the net effect will be to reduce somewhat the earnings gap between college-educated workers and workers with no postsecondary education. In our view this outcome is desirable because, as illustrated in Figure 5.3, this gap has grown markedly over recent decades, and the earnings (net of inflation) of high school graduates have declined. Moreover, unless the percentage of the workforce that is college educated increases, the gap will continue to grow as a result of the changing occupational mix.

Shouldn't schools be doing more than preparing students for work? What about preparing students to be good citizens in a pluralistic democracy?

Of course schools need to do more than prepare students to earn a decent living. However, the stability of our democracy depends on broad-based sharing in the nation's economic benefits. The dramatic changes taking place in the nation's economy jeopardize the economic future for poorly educated students and thereby weaken commitment to the democratic values that underlie our country.

Moreover, technological advances have not only resulted in changes in the economy; they have also created a host of complex social issues. These include deterioration of the environment,

Figure 5.3. Changes in earnings gap between high school and college graduates

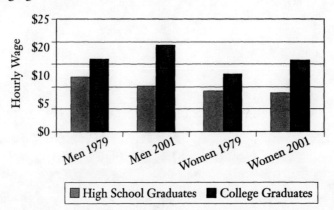

Source: Authors' calculations based on Current Population Surveys conducted by the U.S. Census Bureau.

threats to privacy, and the danger of nuclear holocaust. Dealing with these problems requires a citizenry able to understand complex issues and able to participate in dialogue about the merits of alternative public actions. In other words, complex communication and expert thinking are important skills for contributing to life in a pluralistic democracy.

Note

1. Pellegrino, J., Chudowsky, N., & Glazer, R. (Eds.). (2001). *Knowing what students know: The science and design of educational assessment.* Washington, DC: National Academy Press.

FRANK LEVY *is Daniel Rose Professor of Urban Economics at MIT.*

RICHARD J. MURNANE *is Thompson Professor of Education and Society at the Harvard Graduate School of Education.*

Infusing twenty-first century skills into American education requires a detailed research and development plan for teaching, professional development, and assessment significant to these skills.

6

Establishing the R&D agenda for twenty-first century learning

Ken Kay, Margaret Honey

MUCH INK HAS FLOWED over the past few years describing the need to incorporate twenty-first century skills into K–12 education.[1] As information age and globalization trends have wended their way into the workplace, marketplace, home, government, and community, it has noticeably altered the fundamental life skills expected of citizenry, ratcheted up the demands and expectations of the employers, and introduced powerful forces into the world economy that cut across national borders. Preparing students to succeed as citizens, thinkers, and workers—the bedrock of any educational system—in this environment means arming them with more than a list of facts and important dates. Today's students need critical reasoning, creative, technical, and interpersonal skills to solve complex problems; design new product prototypes; and collaborate across teams and borders using technology as one of their fundamental tools, canvases, or means of communications.

We acknowledge the tremendous contributions of Chad Fasca of the Center for Children and Technology.

Our nation's initial response has focused on how to quickly infuse standards, professional development programs, and assessments with what we already know regarding how to think critically, problem-solve, and communicate and how to use technology to accomplish those skills. This strategy is under way and already bearing fruit in several states and districts.[2]

However, for these skills to gain any traction in the educational system, such interventions need to be complemented by a parallel, longer-term agenda to develop world-class strategies for teaching and assessing the full panoply of twenty-first century skills. Targeted, sustained investment in research and development initiatives is required to elucidate these skills and craft teaching practices and assessment approaches that more closely convey and measure what students need in order for them to excel in the twenty-first century.

The purpose of this chapter is to examine the need for, and future direction of, a twenty-first century skills research and development agenda, specifically:

- The rationale for such a strategy
- The clarity of twenty-first century skills as a primary R&D focus
- The need for an R&D agenda focused on pedagogy
- The need for an R&D agenda focused on assessment
- The implications of this agenda for colleges of education and higher education

We hope that this analysis will spur dialogue within the state and national policymaker communities and in academic communities on the need for a proactive U.S. research agenda in the area of twenty-first century skills.

Rationale: Redefining scholastic rigor in a twenty-first century context

There is little doubt that globalization and information technologies have radically transformed the way we live, learn, and work, positioning our civic and economic lives to unfold in an international context. From Friedman to Prestowitz, the challenge for U.S. citizens and workers is well documented and quite sobering.[3] Our nation's economic leadership position in the world is suddenly in question. Following on the heels of manufacturing jobs, skilled work and high-tech manufacturing are shifting overseas.[4] The United States now has a more than $30 billion high-tech trade deficit, with China accounting for roughly $21 billion of it.

The educational landscape has also tilted, and not in our favor. Our economic competitors in Europe and Asia have recognized the forces at work in the global marketplace and are implementing strategies designed to assist their young people in preparing for the expanding nature of global competition. Rising economic powers such as China and India have made significant strides in closing the sciences and higher education gap. Thirty-eight percent of bachelor's degrees in China were awarded in engineering compared to less than 6 percent in the United States. India in the past decade has increased by 92 percent the number of students enrolled in college.[5] China has made information technology courses compulsory for all its high school students, part of a national information age education plan to train students to be information literate, so that they will be able to collect and analyze information as well as communicate and express it.[6] Singapore has excelled by identifying and continually reevaluating the demands on its workforce and has adjusted its national educational goals, programs, and investments to match the transformation of its economy.[7] In five-year increments, its centralized curriculum, pedagogy, assessment, and educational information and communication technology (ICT) plan has shifted from a focus on the basics—particularly mathematics and science—to a cultivation of creativity and innovation designed to accommodate its growing knowledge economy. In Finland, where decisions on curriculum and instruction are made locally, the government has created policies and programs to support teachers and students in developing knowledge-building skills through student-centered approaches to teaching and learning linked to their communities and local businesses.[8]

We hope this new global reality puts the current education debate in America into a helpful context. Our attempt to ensure that every child has the basics in education is a reasonable starting point for recalibrating American education, but it can only be the starting point. Back to basics or accountability limited to mastery of traditional core subjects will not provide young Americans with the adequate base from which to fend off or excel in the new global competition. In order to assist students in learning the content and skills required to be successful in this new global economy, we as a nation need to expand our efforts to provide a twenty-first century set of educational basics—a basics-plus education—to our children and benchmark these efforts against those of other countries.

In part, this will require a transformation from a sole focus on traditional subject matter mastery to a much higher prioritization of the cross-cutting skills needed to be successful in every enterprise in the twenty-first century. Employers of every kind (for profit and nonprofit) and every type of civic engagement require critical thinking, problem-solving, and effective communications skills.[9]

While other national governments, particularly the United Kingdom, have zeroed in on these learning skills as the key to preparing their students for the twenty-first century, the United States has taken a different tack.[10] In its latest report, the Partnership for 21st Century Skills signaled the shortcomings of this current model: "Many high school reform initiatives aim to keep more students in school, enroll them in more challenging classes, and, as a result, raise high school graduation and college matriculation and retention rates. These are important goals. Yet even if every high school in the country achieved these goals, high school graduates would remain woefully lacking in preparation for the world."[11]

In the U.S. approach, learning skills have often been considered a by-product of effective subject matter teaching. Now they must become the intentional and purposeful outcomes of our education system, which will require a significant shift in current pedagogy and assessment strategies. The real economic advances of this century will be made by societies that produce breakthroughs in the teaching and assessing of critical thinking, problem-solving, and communications skills. Breakthroughs in our understanding of learning and communications will have an impact not only on the education sector, but also on every other sector of the economy, because they will shape the value added by our workforce to everything from how employees are trained to how products and services are created.

We are already seeing dislocations in the global economy where easily routinized and computerized services are being outsourced to countries that can provide these services the most efficiently (see Chapter Five, this volume). This offshoring puts even more pressure on our society to produce higher value-added products and services not easily outsourced. In the global economy, this requires investment in finding ways for our education system to produce learners who can effectively bring added value to their employers, industries, and society.

To underscore the importance of this general line of R&D investment, it is worthwhile to consider John Bransford's work on adaptive learning.[12] He makes the observation that our current educational system is still primarily focused on a model that teaches every child something a hundred times and measures their ability to produce the same answer the 101st time. He observes that the real focus now needs to be on measuring a student's ability to address a problem he or she has never seen before. Economic success will come to those societies that teach students to address new problems, which Bransford refers to as adaptive learning.

Our academic research has focused primarily on traditional subject matter inquiry because we have defined academic rigor as the rigor of specific subject matter expertise. In the twenty-first century, we will need a new definition of rigor that recognizes that each student must possess the ability to apply critical twenty-first century skills to their understanding of all subjects. This goal requires a rethinking of what we are focused on in education, and the resulting new emphasis will have profound implications for a research agenda:

- Do we understand how to define twenty-first century learning?
- Do we understand the key elements that comprise twenty-first century learning?
- Do we know how to most effectively teach twenty-first century learning?
- Do we know how to most effectively assess twenty-first century learning?

These questions alone would constitute a robust research agenda. But they are only a small portion of the questions that need to be pursued. There is a broad agenda of twenty-first century skills that requires substantial research and development.

The twenty-first century skills framework as an R&D focus

Although several frameworks have been developed over the past fifteen years to increase our attention to workforce issues,[13] none is as comprehensive for these purposes as the one developed by the Partnership for 21st Century Skills.[14] The value of the partnership's framework is that it builds on the traditional context of core subjects and offers four additional areas:

- Thinking and learning skills
- ICT literacy skills
- Life skills
- Twenty-first century content

How do we produce the highest level of analytical thinking in all of our students? How do we produce the highest level of problem solving in all students? How do we produce the highest level of innovation skills in all students? These are new areas of inquiry that represent the core of a strategic agenda for research. We suggest the R&D agenda for twenty-first century skills generally tracks the framework developed by the partnership.

Thinking, learning, and innovation skills are probably the most important set of skills to focus on from an R&D agenda perspective. Among the questions that would drive this agenda are these:

- How can students take ownership of developing and tracking their analytical thinking and problem-solving skills?
- How do students become truly innovative learners?
- How do we most effectively teach and measure self-directed learning skills?

We are often asked whether these skills are in lieu of content mastery. The answer is no. These skills cannot be taught in a vacuum. They must be taught in the context of subject matter. The subject matter is the medium in which the skills are exercised and honed, but the skills are what students should attempt to attain. Most students will spend their lives in and out of subjects and combinations of subjects. Much of the time, they will not have mastered the specific subject but will be called on to apply the skill set that they have acquired across a range of subjects.

The second set of skills is ICT literacy: the ability to use technology to accomplish learning, thinking, and innovation skills. We are just at the beginning of creating the tools to teach and assess ICT literacy. The key focus of this literacy is not technology competency but the ability to use technology to perform critical thinking, problem-solving, collaboration, communication, and innovation skills. This area of R&D will support all enterprises and every category of the workforce and stands to bear the most fruit.

The final skills category comprises life skills: interpersonal and collaborative, self-direction and productivity, adaptability, responsibility and accountability, leadership, and career awareness skills. More and more, employers are finding these skills are central to the success of employees. Cultures that consider the overall education system and how technology contributes to these skills will put themselves at a competitive advantage. For example, personal productivity (time management, multitasking) is a particularly important individual attribute in the twenty-first century. Little is currently known about how to foster personal productivity. But as the education system develops over the next two decades, the infusion of personal productivity into K–12 education and pedagogical strategies will likely be an important component of effective education.

It is our hope that this brief introduction to the twenty-first century skills framework outlines the building blocks and research questions that can be used to guide an approach to infusing these skills into teaching, professional development, and assessment at every level of the education system.

The need for an R&D agenda focused on pedagogy

One of the linchpins to a successful transformation of our educational system will be the ability to fully ascertain the most effective ways to teach twenty-first century skills and build these strategies into a revamped system of professional development. Much has been made in recent years of how U.S. students compare to their international counterparts. Results from the 2003 Trends in International Mathematics and Science Study (TIMSS), which measures core curriculum content learning, have received significant press attention. These results show that mathematics performance among U.S. eighth-grade students lags behind that of fourteen other countries.[15]

Recent reforms such as the No Child Left Behind Act have sought to correct this deficit with a focus on core content standards and high-stakes assessments tied to federal and state funding.[16] However, while we confine our perspective on teaching and learning to the acquisition and demonstration of factual knowledge in core subjects, our economic competitors in Europe and Asia are focusing on newer forms of assessment, particularly the Programme for International Student Assessment (PISA), that measure how students (in this case, fifteen year olds) apply what they have learned (reading, mathematics, and science content knowledge and skills) to analyzing and evaluating information and solving problems and issues in real-life contexts.[17] Thirty countries, including the United States, participated in the assessment's first application in 2003. U.S. students, who appear near the middle of the pack on TIMSS, rank in the bottom third of PISA, trailing their competitors in twenty-first century learning: applying knowledge in real-world contexts. Failing to address this issue head on through investments in research and professional development puts our students at risk of obsolescence.

Pointing out the critical importance of teacher professional development to achievement, Sparks and Hersh wrote, "If states want teachers to radically change their results to get all students achieving, they must give teachers the tools, support, and training to radically change their practice. America cannot climb past its current achievement plateau without educating teachers, administrators, and other educators on what they need to do to reach the higher levels."[18]

We need well-researched strategies and best practices for teaching twenty-first century skills. States must take a leadership role in guiding comprehensive reforms through their composite educational systems, including establishing professional development initiatives that prepare teachers to teach the full range of skills using the best practices available. Without a clearly defined, comprehensive professional development strategy, there is little doubt that twenty-first century skills reform will fall short. Research into identifying best practices and training teachers to use these approaches is critical to the long-term viability of twenty-first century skills in education.

We are not without examples of reform efforts tied to professional development programs. Led by their respective governors, North Carolina and West Virginia are implementing the model for teaching and learning promoted by the Partnership for 21st Century Skills. North Carolina is establishing a public-private statewide advocacy institution, the North Carolina Center for 21st Century Skills, to ensure that students graduate from the state's educational institutions with the skills needed to compete in today's marketplace, and it has linked its activities with the state's professional development academy. West Virginia has just launched an initiative to promote professional development in twenty-first century teaching at both higher education teacher preparation institutions and at the classroom level to review current education standards to ensure the inclusion of twenty-first century skills and to align assessments with twenty-first century learning outcomes. Lawrence Township (Indianapolis) has underpinned its efforts to introduce twenty-first century skills into its schools with a strong professional development strategy.

These and other leading-edge practices need to be studied so that we can determine the most effective strategies for teacher preparation. Our experience suggests that reforms will succeed only when closely aligned with teacher professional development. Without a research agenda focused on identifying the best practices in teaching twenty-first century skills and the best models for delivering the professional development necessary to bring these practices to classrooms nationwide, any reforms we enact will lack foundation.

"Of all the stakeholders . . . to prepare today's children for tomorrow's world," Dede, Korte, Valdez, and Ward write, "the single most important group is teachers. No educational improvement effort can succeed without building teachers' capacity to innovate."[19]

The need for an assessment strategy R&D agenda

While much importance must be placed on understanding the most effective pedagogical strategies, the entire pipeline of education will be profoundly affected by major breakthroughs in the assessment of twenty-first century skills. These breakthroughs need to be made in large-scale assessments as well as classroom assessments. Describing the role of assessment in pedagogical reform, Yeh wrote, "If one accepts the premise that tests drive curriculum and instruction, perhaps the easiest way to reform instruction and improve educational quality is to construct better tests."[20] Assessment is the tail that wags the dog.

Since many of today's high-stakes tests focus primarily on the recall of factual knowledge and vocabulary, U.S. teachers have followed suit by narrowing the curriculum and their instructional practice to memorization, drills, practice tests, and worksheets designed to improve their students' achievement on core content knowledge. Despite an understanding at the classroom level and the business community that critical thinking, problem-solving, and communication skills are vital to students' future success, teachers have little time to address these skills. With appropriate assessments of twenty-first century skills in place, teachers would have the opportunity to cover this critical area in their classrooms. Klein, Kuh, Chun, Hamilton, and Shavelson suggest that new measures of critical thinking skills will be more sensitive to program and institutional effects than are traditional tests of general educational abilities.[21]

Yeh outlines four basic principles for constructing tests of critical thinking: (1) determine whether children can use instead of just recall facts, (2) make available evidence that is open to alternative interpretations, (3) ask respondents to explain what effect changes in evidence, such as faulty or new evidence being uncovered, would have on their answers, and (4) probe content knowledge appropriate in a real-world context.[22]

Within the past several years, assessments have been developed in the United States and United Kingdom that attempt to capture students' ability to apply learning skills to solving real-world problems. The Collegiate Learning Assessment (CLA) measures critical reasoning competencies without assessing ICT use (ICT is used only as a test delivery and scoring mechanism). ETS's ICT Literacy Assessment and the United Kingdom's Key Stage 3 ICT Onscreen Test measure students' higher-order competencies through ICT use.

"The use of ICT in assessment is the most powerful lever available to embed the government's e-learning and ICT initiatives in the classroom, as assessment defines the goals for both learners and teachers," according to Martin Ripley, director of e-assessment strategy for the British government's Qualifications and Curriculum Authority (personal communication to the authors, 2005).

Although each assessment is designed for slightly different purposes and audiences, each shares a core element: they invite students to apply their twenty-first century learning skills to the investigation and resolution of a genuine problem, such as completing a sales presentation, researching and reporting on diversity in the local government of a virtual town, or analyzing and selecting for purchase important equipment for a business.

The CLA and ICT assessments are currently geared toward the college level, though earlier application is either planned or possible. CLA compares baseline data on incoming freshmen with data on outgoing seniors to examine the impact that colleges and universities have on students' acquisition of critical reasoning skills. The ETS assessment focuses on providing colleges, universities, and companies with information on the ICT proficiency levels of incoming or advancing students.

The U.K. Qualifications and Curriculum Authority has made a substantial investment in its Key Stage 3 ICT Onscreen Test (roughly $45 million), which will serve a dual role: a national system to gauge overall effectiveness in teaching ICT literacy to students approaching high school age and a formative tool kit available 365 days a year for classroom- and school-based assessments.

With spending on assessment development expected to reach $3.9 billion according to government estimates,[23] it is vital that we direct these resources to new assessment tools modeled using the Key Stage 3, CLA, ICT literacy assessment, and other leading assessments of twenty-first century skills. Fulfilling current federal requirements for new assessments is not enough and will leave us precariously short of preparing children to succeed. With assessment as a key driver of reform efforts, we need to align measurement tools with classroom objectives.

To track developments in this critical field, the Partnership for 21st Century Skills has created a database of skills assessments, dubbed Assess 21, to serve as a central hub for policymakers, educators, researchers, and others seeking background information on current assessments of twenty-first century skills. The repository, which is open to assessment developer submission, seeks to highlight assessments of twenty-first century skills as they become available. It breaks down assessments across a number of categories, including grade group, twenty-first century skill, assessment format, impetus (policy, commercial, noncommercial), region of origin, and administration method. Tracking what is happening in both the United States and abroad is critical to developing sound strategies and tools for measuring twenty-first century skills.

As we noted at the outset, to truly ascertain where our students, our education system, and its components (for example, professional development and assessment) stand today, we will need to monitor international developments in these areas carefully. In some areas, such as the assessment of ICT literacy, the U.K. government is clearly ahead of the rest of the world. Our own R&D agenda needs to take into account these kinds of international developments, carefully determine what breakthroughs are being made globally, and measure our own progress against them. Only when we benchmark our own efforts to teach and assess twenty-first century skills against the efforts of our competitors can we ensure that our students receive the best possible preparation for the new global economy.

Critical role of higher education and colleges of education

Twenty years ago, the business and education communities recognized the dismal state of business schools. State-of-the-art business practices such as just-in-time manufacturing and Total Quality Management were not included in their curricula. Following some hand wringing, business schools instituted major reforms to help their graduates attain skills that were required to sustain the transformation going on in the business sector.

Today colleges of education and other areas of higher education responsible for teacher preparation face no less a crisis. They need to respond no less dramatically by adopting the teaching and assessment of twenty-first century skills as a major part of their

NEW DIRECTIONS FOR YOUTH DEVELOPMENT • DOI: 10.1002/yd

research and teaching missions. Every board of regents, university chancellor, and president needs to take on this assignment and swiftly reengineer the teaching, learning, and research functions of their colleges of education and teacher preparation programs to embrace this critical research agenda. In fact, teacher preparation programs should be at the forefront of R&D on twenty-first century skills.

Given the emerging importance of workforce preparation and training, the priority of research in education and training must be brought to the forefront of academic quality. We should be urging and enticing our best students into this field of research. We must convey that the intersection of education and other critical disciplines, such as cognitive psychology and information technology, is among the most important areas of research in the next twenty years.

We must acknowledge the addition of new content areas that are critical for students' future success in the global economy and society at large. The Partnership for 21st Century Skills has identified several critical subjects that often do not receive adequate attention in either state standards or implementation:

- Global and cultural awareness
- Civic engagement
- Business, financial, and economic literacy
- Health and wellness

These are content areas in varying degrees of development, but the business and education communities are in agreement that they merit inclusion in twenty-first century education. Colleges of education should be working with the other relevant disciplines to develop content and pedagogical strategies to teach these subjects at all appropriate age levels. But we cannot expect expanding the roster of subject matter alone to produce the qualities that students need in the information age without simultaneously addressing critical thinking and problem-solving skills.

NEW DIRECTIONS FOR YOUTH DEVELOPMENT • DOI: 10.1002/yd

The ability of states to require critical thinking and problem-solving skills depends on the creation of tools to teach and measure them. Leadership from the academic community is required to help design a path that educational professionals can follow in order to help their students meet the challenges that the future economy will present. Each day that goes by without making serious reforms in colleges of education means that we continue to send new teachers into the classroom without the skills they need to adequately prepare their students for their future challenges.

The Elementary and Secondary Education Act clearly states, "Almost all practicing educators and their teachers have learned their craft using 20th century decision-making models. Our society should undertake an intentional, large-scale transition creating the capacity for current and new educators to lead communities and the nation toward the future, not to reinforce their past. The nation should infuse new models for teaching and learning based upon effective research-based models."[24]

The best way to make this transition is to have university professors and their preservice students engaged in exploring, implementing, and testing twenty-first century learning strategies. If the society needs every student to be an analytical thinker, problem solver, innovative learner, self-directed learner, and effective communicator and to be ICT literate, then colleges of education should be at the forefront of determining how best to teach and assess these skills. Teacher education programs represent a critical vehicle for modeling and establishing twenty-first century practices. Each institution needs to craft a teaching agenda that includes continual evaluations of what tools and skills teachers need in order to create information age classrooms that foster twenty-first century learning, a research plan for charting the best practices for teaching and assessing twenty-first century skills, and an overall commitment to ensure that all preservice teachers graduate prepared to employ twenty-first century teaching and assessment strategies in their classrooms.

Conclusion

Just as reading, writing, and arithmetic are essential for any student to succeed regardless of career, education, research, and innovation are essential if the nation is to succeed in providing jobs for its citizenry.[25]

Research has always been the fundamental investment that we can make to ensure the long-term success of critical enterprises. While we pursue shorter-term tactics to identify underperforming schools and districts, we also need to embrace the next generation of educational goals and strategies.

We are fortunate that a growing consensus has developed among business and education leaders on which skills and content areas are central to student success in civic and economic life. This twenty-first century skills framework should not only guide our short-term consideration of such critical subjects as accountability and high school reform, but equally important, provide the construct for a longer-term investment in the research that will position us at the forefront of creating a highly competitive twenty-first century citizenry and workforce.

By focusing our research agenda on how best to teach and assess twenty-first century skills, the nation will be positioning itself and each of its citizens for long-term success in the emerging global competition.

Notes

1. Dede, C., Korte, S., Valdez, G., & Ward, D. J. (2005, September). *Transforming learning for the twenty-first century: An economic imperative.* Naperville, IL: Learning Points Associates. http://www.learningpt.org/tech/transforming.pdf; Kay, K., & Honey, M. (2005). *Beyond technology competency: A vision of ICT literacy to prepare students for the twenty-first century.* Charleston, WV: Edvantia; Partnership for 21st Century Skills. (2003). *Learning for the twenty-first century.* Washington, DC: Author. http://www.21stcenturyskills.org/images/stories/otherdocs/P21_Report.pdf; Partnership for 21st Century Skills. (2005). *Road to twenty-first century learning: A policymaker's guide to twenty-first century skills.* Washington, DC: Author. http://www.21stcenturyskills.org/images/stories/otherdocs/P21_Policy_Paper.pdf; Levy, F., & Murnane, R. J. (2004). *The new division of labor: How computers are creating the next labor market.* Princeton, NJ: Princeton University Press; Ber-

telsmann Foundation and AOL Time Warner Foundation. (2002, March). *Twenty-first century literacy in a convergent media world.* White paper from the Twenty-First Century Literacy Summit: Berlin. www.twenty-firstcentury literacy.org.; ETS: International ICT Literacy Panel. (2001). *Digital transformation: A framework for ICT literacy.* Princeton, NJ: Educational Testing Service. www.ets.org/research/ictliteracy/index.html.

2. North Carolina and West Virginia recently announced plans to revise state education policy to include language that reflects the addition of twenty-first century learning skills as an expectation for teaching and learning in each state.

3. Friedman, T. (2005). *The world is flat.* New York: Farrar, Straus and Giroux; Prestowitz, C. (2005). *Three billion new capitalists: The great shift of wealth and power to the East.* New York: Basic Books.

4. Programming jobs are heading overseas by the thousands. Is there a way for the U.S. to stay on top? (2004, March 1). *Business Week;* Gartner: More U.S. IT jobs heading overseas. (2003, July 30). *Silicon Valley/San Jose Business Journal.* http://www.bizjournals.com/sanjose/stories/2003/07/28/daily29.html.

5. Spellings, M. (2005, May 6). *Is America really serious about educating every child?* Prepared remarks for the Education Writers Association National Seminar, St. Petersburg, FL. http://www.ed.gov/news/speeches/2005/05/05062005.html.

6. Feicheng, M., & Cuihua, H. (2002, July). *Information literacy, education reform and the economy: China as a case study.* White Paper prepared for UNESCO, the U.S. National Commission on Libraries and Information Science, and the National Forum on Information Literacy, for use at the Information Literacy Meeting of Experts, Prague, Czech Republic. http://www.nclis.gov/libinter/infolitconf&meet/papers/ma-fullpaper.pdf.

7. Kozma, R. B. (2005). National policies that connect ICT-based education reform to economic and social development. *Human Technology, 1,* 117–156.

8. Kozma. (2005).

9. Meisinger, S. (2004, November). Shortage of skilled workers threatens economy. *HR Magazine.*

10. Kelly, R. (2005, July 13). *Creating a world class workforce—the government's view.* Speech at the Skills Summit Conference, QEII Conference Centre, London. http://www.dfes.gov.uk/skillsstrategy/_pdfs/whitePaper_PDFID121.pdf; White House. (2004, January 21). *Fact sheet: Jobs in the twenty-first century.* http://www.whitehouse.gov/news/releases/2004/01/20040121.html.

11. Partnership for 21st Century Skills. (2006, March). *Results that matter: 21st century skills in high school reform.* Washington, DC: Author.

12. Bransford, J., Brown, A., & Cocking, R. (2000). *How people learn: Brain, mind, experience and school.* Washington, DC: National Academy Press.

13. U.S. Department of Labor (1991). *What work requires of schools: A SCANS report for America 2000.* Washington, DC: Secretary's Commission on Achieving Necessary Skills; Business-Higher Education Forum. (1999). *Spanning the chasm: A blueprint for action.* Washington, DC: American Council of Education/National Alliance of Business.

14. Partnership for 21st Century Skills. (2003); Partnership for 21st Century Skills. (2005)

15. Mullis, I.V.S., Martin, M. O., Gonzalez, E. J., & Chrostowski, S. J. (2004). *TIMMS 2003 international mathematics report.* Chestnut Hill, MA: TIMSS and PIRLS International Study Center, Boston College.

16. Elementary and Secondary Education Act. (2001). *No Child Left Behind Act of 2001.* http://www.ed.gov/policy/elsec/leg/esea02/index.html.

17. Stage, E. K. (2005, Winter). Why do we need these assessments? *Natural Selection: Journal of BSCS,* 11–13.

18. Sparks, D., & Hirsh, S. (1999). *A national plan for improving professional development.* Oxford, OH: National Staff Development Council. http://www. nsdc.org/library/authors/NSDCPlan.cfm.

19. Dede et al. (2005, September).

20. Yeh, S. (2001, December). Tests worth teaching to: Constructing state-mandated tests that emphasize critical thinking. *Educational Researcher, 30*(9), 12–17.

21. Klein, S., Kuh, G., Chun, M., Hamilton, L., & Shavelson, R. (2003, April). *The search for value-added: Assessing and validating selected higher education outcomes.* Paper presented at the 84th Annual Meeting of the American Educational Research Association, Chicago.

22. Yeh. (2001).

23. Government Accounting Office. (2003, May). *Title I characteristics of tests will influence expenses; information sharing may help states realize efficiencies.* Washington, DC: Author.

24. Elementary and Secondary Education Act. (2001).

25. Committee on Prospering in the Global Economy in the Twenty-First Century: An Agenda for American Science and Technology. (2005). *Rising above the gathering storm: Energizing and employing America for a brighter economic future.* Washington, DC: National Academies Press.

KEN KAY *is president of the Partnership for 21st Century Skills, America's leading advocacy organization focused on infusing twenty-first century skills into education.*

MARGARET HONEY *is vice president of the Education Development Center and director of its Center for Children and Technology, which investigates the roles that technology can play in improving teaching and learning inside and outside the classroom.*

NEW DIRECTIONS FOR YOUTH DEVELOPMENT • DOI: 10.1002/yd

Afterschool represents a vast opportunity to reimagine education, building twenty-first century skills among students beyond the traditional six-hour school day.

7

Twenty-first century learning in afterschool

Eric Schwarz, David Stolow

AFTER-SCHOOL PROGRAMS offer a superb venue to teach twenty-first century skills. Students in these programs work in small teams. They investigate, analyze, synthesize, experiment, and reflect. The programs enable students to explore new fields, use new technology, meet real-world challenges, and develop mastery. They create a new civic space in which young people can forge positive relationships with adults, learn the joys of productive work, and be recognized as contributors to their communities. Indeed, when we refocus our lens from school reform to education reform, we see after-school programs emerging as one of the nation's most promising strategies for developing twenty-first century skills.

Despite this promise, the vast potential for after-school programs to help transform American education remains mostly unrecognized and untapped. The after-school sector is fragmented and lacks a consistent identity, structure, pedagogy, or delivery mechanism. It has not delivered compelling results at significant scale.[1] But these weaknesses need not be debilitating or permanent. Pursuing reform *within* schools also presents stubborn obstacles. What

NEW DIRECTIONS FOR YOUTH DEVELOPMENT, NO. 110, SUMMER 2006 © WILEY PERIODICALS, INC.
Published online in Wiley InterScience (www.interscience.wiley.com) • DOI: 10.1002/yd.169

81

is needed is a comprehensive strategy that looks to build twenty-first century skills within the traditional six-hour school day as well as within the vast landscape of out-of-school time—the four thousand hours of afternoon, evening, weekend, and vacation time when American children are awake but not in school.

This chapter examines the current and potential role of after-school programs in building twenty-first century skills—a set of competencies well defined elsewhere in this volume that include creativity, using data to solve complex problems, nuanced oral and written communication, and the ability to work well on diverse teams. We present examples, research, and expert testimonials that suggest the power of out-of-school learning to boost twenty-first century skills. But first it is helpful to set a framework for why this topic is so important.

The urgent challenge of teaching twenty-first century skills

Are twenty-first century skills really so important? Yes, and the simplest reason is economics. We live in a fast-changing global economy in which jobs that require workers to repeat physical or mental activities or follow a prescribed set of rules (jobs requiring twentieth-century skills) have been computerized, sent offshore, or remain in the United States but offer lower wages because anyone can do them (see Chapter Five, this volume). In the future, there will be more retail and fast food jobs that do not require twenty-first century skills but that also will not pay well. Fortunately, there will also be growing numbers of blue-collar and white-collar jobs that do pay well. But these jobs will require twenty-first century skills.[2] Simply put, twenty-first century skills are now the ticket to enter the middle class.

There are at least two additional reasons that twenty-first century skills are important. First, we believe the new workforce skills of teamwork, use of data to solve problems, creativity, and nuanced communication are also the skills citizens needed to reinvigorate civic life and participate in public debate. Second, jobs requiring twenty-first century skills are more likely to be fulfilling and fun, not just better paying. As Daniel Pink explained in his book *A Whole New Mind: Moving from the Information Age to the Conceptual Age*, as computers and workers abroad take over more jobs involving repetition, there will be more jobs in the United States requiring creativity, imagination, and collaborative work.[3]

If we agree that twenty-first century skills are vital—and this has been consensus among education leaders at least since *A Nation at Risk* was published in 1983—then how well are we teaching them?[4] Not well. Over the past twenty-five years, American elementary school children have made modest gains in basic reading and math skills. Middle school children have made some gains in math but not in reading skills, and high school students have not made gains in either area.[5] And during this same period, the communication and problem-solving skills of American children appear to have declined, or at least stagnated. Writing scores on the National Assessment of Educational Progress (NAEP) declined through most of the 1980s and 1990s. A recent study indicated that the literacy skills of college graduates declined from 1992 to 2003. The NAEP data on writing achievement shows that writing levels declined modestly for eighth graders and steeply for eleventh graders from 1984 to 1996, while fourth graders showed a modest increase during the same period.[6] At the same time, American public school children continue to score very low on international assessments that test problem-solving skills. In 2003, for instance, U.S. fifteen year olds ranked in the bottom third of thirty countries tested in the Programme for International Student Assessment of problem-solving abilities in math and science.[7]

In *Teaching the New Basic Skills*, Murnane and Levy took the ambitious step of interviewing dozens of employers to discover exactly what skills they required of their entry-level workers. They discovered first that employers used a sophisticated battery of assessments. These included multiple-choice tests, writing assessments, interviews, and even psychological profiles. They summarized that the new basic skills required to get a middle-class job were basic skills in the three R's; the ability to work on a diverse team; the ability to use data to solve semistructured problems; the ability to use computers as a tool; and the ability to communicate effectively in writing and orally. Then Murnane and Levy went further. They compared the actual skills of high school graduates to the desired profile described by the employers. Their conclusion was that half of all high school graduates, presumably including many with solid grade point averages who passed standardized tests, did not have the new basic skills. They were no longer employable in a middle-class job.[8]

Howard Gardner makes a similar point in his seminal book *The Unschooled Mind.* He argues that traditional schools give students enough basic knowledge to answer standard questions correctly, particularly in a multiple-choice format. But the students' knowledge is "fragile." The same student who knows enough to generate what Gardner calls "correct answer compromises" and get the right answer on simple tests may not know enough to apply the relevant knowledge in new ways. These students have learned a twentieth-century skill (repeating a problem-solving strategy or summarizing basic information) but have not mastered the twenty-first century skill of applying deep knowledge to solve new problems or to convey a nuanced point of view.[9]

This challenge is heightened in states with simplistic assessments. In Massachusetts and other states where high-stakes tests require students to solve problems, show their work, and write essays, students are more likely to build twenty-first century skills. But studies by the American Federation of Teachers and by Achieve, the education reform group, indicate that more than half of all states limit their high-stakes assessments entirely or almost entirely to multiple-choice tests that assess basic skills but not higher order thinking.[10] What gets measured is what gets done. Unfortunately, far too many school systems are measuring and teaching skills that were adequate in the past but will not be in the future.

We believe there are at least four reasons that schools alone are not building the twenty-first century skills students need:

NEW DIRECTIONS FOR YOUTH DEVELOPMENT • DOI: 10.1002/yd

1. Limits of time. Traditional schools serve students for only about one thousand hours a year (180 days, 6 hours a day)—not enough time to build both basic reading and math skills *and* higher-level twenty-first century skills, particularly if students start the year behind grade level and if these skills are not regularly reinforced at home or in after-school programs.

2. Limits of structure. School buildings and most classrooms have a set physical size. Traditional classrooms—with one teacher and twenty-five to thirty students, each at desks—discourage the type of small group activities and off-site projects that are ideal for building twenty-first century skills.

3. Limits of inertia and bureaucracy. As the past twenty years have amply demonstrated and as academics such as Richard Elmore and David Cohen have described,[11] schools and school districts are entrenched organisms that are resistant to change (M. Tierney, personal communication, January 2004). Changing from a basic skills agenda to a new basic skills approach is difficult.

4. Limits of priorities. The standards movement, which may have reached its apex with the No Child Left Behind (NCLB) Act of 2001, requires schools to focus their energy on the basics. While many great teachers and a handful of great schools have been able to embed high-level basic skill development into projects that also build twenty-first century skills (see Chapters Eight and Nine, this volume), most have chosen to devote more time to basic math and basic reading and have not made time to also focus on a twenty-first century skills agenda.

The last of these reasons deserves a little more discussion. The accountability provisions of NCLB are likely to be the driving force of education reform for years to come. Are we suggesting that twenty-first century skills should become the sole NCLB standard and that we should do away with tests measuring basic skills? Certainly not. Basic skills remain the bedrock of success, but they are not enough. What we need is a challenging in- and out-of-school curriculum that embeds the basics in higher-order learning activities. And we need to broaden what schools are accountable for to include twenty-first century skills (see Chapter Six, this volume).

To summarize, twenty-first century skills are now necessary for most middle-class jobs and helpful in civic life as well. Despite the importance of these skills, about half of high school graduates lack them, and many American youth are falling further behind their peers in other countries. One reason for this predicament, we believe, is that many schools have not focused on twenty-first century learning, in part because of institutional restraints of time, structure, bureaucracy, and priorities.

The special role after-school programs can play in teaching twenty-first century skills

Afterschool is no panacea. The field has its own challenges. But afterschool is a relative blank slate and offers several relative advantages in building twenty-first century skills. Done right, out-of-school learning offers more of what we all want from education: discovery, small learning teams, real-world skills, character development, and wonder. What is ideal, we believe, is a reimagined school day that includes more time for learning the old basic skills as well as more time and space for the type of small group, real-world activities that are likely to build twenty-first century skills. We believe high-quality after-school programs are well positioned to build twenty-first century skills for three mains reasons:

- They operate in small groups that require teamwork.
- They are well suited for project-based learning and offer superb opportunities for students to develop mastery.
- They can offer real-world learning that is meaningful to students because it engages the broader community.

Small group size

A core twenty-first century skill is the ability to work on a small, diverse team, share ideas, and solve problems. This is the workforce of the future. But participating in teams effectively takes practice. How do you navigate between listening and sharing your own views? How can you capitalize on the strengths of particular team members? How do you balance planning time with work time? How do you include teammates with lower skill levels without compromising excellence?

The best after-school programs practice teamwork regularly. Adult-to-child ratios are one-to-ten or even one-to-five rather than one-to-twenty-five or worse, as in traditional school-day classrooms. In West Virginia, elementary school participants in one after-school program collected data that tracked pollution levels in local streams and made presentations to legislators about how to solve the problem. The gathering of the data, the forming and the testing of hypotheses as to what the data meant, the drafting and redrafting of letters about the problem, and the imagining of solutions all happened in small group discussions of six to seven students with a young educator facilitating and coaching.[12]

At the National Foundation for Teaching Entrepreneurship, business coaches come together after school with teams of high school students and coach them through a process of developing a product, researching the market, refining the product, raising capital, and then developing and executing a sales strategy. The model relies on a mix of volunteers (real businesspeople) and paid educators and involves teams of five to eight young people with one adult.[13]

At Citizen Schools, the national after-school program for middle school children where we work, all the learning takes place in small teams. Students participate in a "home-room" team of ten to twelve students led by a trained team leader. The team leader coaches students with homework, leads field trips to colleges and museums, and teaches a curriculum specifically designed to build teamwork skills, planning skills, and school navigation skills.

Clearly projects and activities like these can and do take place in some schools. At the best schools, small group projects mix with direct instruction to yield deep student understanding. But our observation of the more than thirty public middle schools that we have worked with (mostly big-city schools serving low-income children) tells us that small group work on authentic projects is too rare in the classroom. Discipline challenges, traditional physical structures, the limit of time, and the core challenge of one adult being responsible for twenty-five to thirty young people usually make it too difficult.

Project-based learning and the opportunity to develop mastery

From John Dewey forward, progressive educational theorists and practitioners have believed that students learn best when they learn by doing.[14] Students need to be engaged in relevant activities where they can test alternative approaches and see the results of their efforts. The Partnership for 21st Century Skills, a consortium of major technology corporations, emphasizes, "Students need to learn academic content through real-world examples, applications and experience both inside and outside of schools. Students understand and retain more when their learning is relevant, engaging, and meaningful to their lives."[15] At Citizen Schools we use the learning triangle: a graphical depiction of the principle that retention of knowledge increases as students hear, see, discuss, do, and teach back (Figure 7.1).

Several education scholars have suggested that project-based approaches, which are especially well suited to the after-school set-

Figure 7.1. The learning triangle

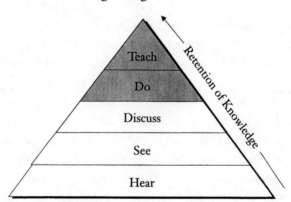

ting, are an effective way to build higher-order thinking skills. Columbia University scholar Lauren Resnick, for instance, argues that a key feature of programs that successfully teach thinking, learning, and higher-order problem solving is that "they are organized around joint accomplishment of tasks, so that elements of skills take on meaning in the context of the whole."[16]

As with small group learning, project-based approaches can be used during the in-school hours, and at the best schools they are. But in most schools that serve low-income students, hands-on projects are the rare exception and far outside the core strategy for teaching and learning. And where project-based learning does happen well, educational leaders find themselves relying on their after-school partners to deepen the learning that begins in the school day. "Just the additional time helps everyone. Practice makes perfect," says Cheryl Bracco, principal of the award-winning McKinley Institute of Technology, a Citizen Schools partner in Redwood City, California. "Because we have a standards based curriculum and because many students need to be accelerated, we don't often have time to do more creative learning that students really need. Citizen Schools fills that gap for us. For example, we did a literacy magazine as one of our apprenticeships, so there was an opportunity for students to write and be creative. Citizen Schools brings the fun of learning into the mix and is able to do activities with students that are outside the box" (J. Cascarino, personal communication, March 2005).

Cognitive apprenticeship experts Allan Collins, John Seely Brown, and Ann Holum concur that cooperative work forces students to articulate to each other their understanding of the materials, and, they say, "gives students practice in the kind of collaboration prevalent in real-world problem solving."[17]

The centrality of practice, and its connection to mastery, is another underappreciated strength of the after-school venue. In *Teaching the New Basic Skills*, Murnane and Levy describe a fabulously instructive episode at a Honda assembly plant. A small team of assembly line workers was given responsibility for solving a small but crucial production problem: the blower nuts they installed in car heaters were getting stuck and could not be fastened securely.

The team, which named itself the Sharpshooters, was given a clear mandate to come up with a solution that would eliminate stopped blower nuts. In a highly structured, methodical process, the Sharpshooters analyzed the sources of the problem, compiled data and displayed them graphically, formulated potential solutions, and tested their proposals under actual plant conditions. And time and again they failed. Each time they reviewed their results, revised their hypothesis, and tried again. After eight months and six iterations of the process, the Sharpshooters got it right, and their new process for installing blower nuts was implemented not only at their plant but across the entire company.[18]

Murnane and Levy use this anecdote to illustrate the way forward-thinking corporations approach learning and professional development for their employees, as well as to underscore employers' demands for twenty-first century skills. At the same time, the story of Honda's Sharpshooters highlights the special capacity of after-school programs: the chance for students to develop mastery. Just as the team at Honda went through several iterations before completing its project (and those many attempts surely heightened the pride they took in their final achievement), so too can students in after-school programs practice their new skills and develop mastery in them. Murnane and Levy write, "We believe high-quality after-school programs can play important roles in helping students develop essential skills for the new economy. Students only acquire expert thinking, complex communication, and other new basic skills by practicing them. After-school programs can provide students opportunities to practice these skills both individually and on teams and to apply them to areas of possible interest."[19]

After-school programs can allow students to learn iteratively and stick with a skill so that they get really good at it. While the new skills they learn might be important, the experience of mastery, regardless of the skill, surely is. Today's students are accustomed to surfing from subject to subject, from one quiz to the next, in the inexorable quest to complete the curriculum before the next round of high-stakes tests. They need to balance breadth with depth. When they go deep in their after-school programs, students recognize that they can apply their learning from one situation to the next, overcome obstacles, and become experts. They learn the skills of analysis and synthesis; see the benefits of communication, teamwork, and perseverance; and experience the well-deserved pride that comes from a job done well.

For far too many students, school is a place where they fail. Afterschool can be a place where they succeed. Countless times at Citizen Schools, we have seen a student who is struggling in the traditional classroom shine in our after-school program. And success in the after-school setting can transform all aspects of the child's life. It changes they way parents and teachers view the child's abilities and relate to the child, the child's approach to schoolwork, and the way the child thinks about herself and her future. At a time when 50 percent of low-income students do not graduate from high school, and half who do graduate lack twenty-first century skills, we need to develop alternative learning environments that give students experiences of success and mastery.

Real-world learning that is meaningful to students and engages the broader community

The new 3 R's of American education are rigor, relevance, and relationships.[20] After-school programs have a special capacity to forge relationships between young people and adults from diverse backgrounds. In doing so, they can introduce students to new disciplines and professions and inspire a zest for learning that will carry over into all domains of a student's life. At the same time, they can give American adults an opportunity to contribute to the learning and healthy development of young people in their communities. As they reengage in the educational process, adults will reconnect with their communities and further their own learning.[21]

As with hands-on learning, there are surely opportunities for traditional schools to engage adult volunteers. But sadly, most do not. Large urban school districts are difficult for prospective volunteers to navigate and notoriously unreceptive to volunteers. Citizen Schools works with countless museums, nonprofits, companies, and individual volunteers who have tried unsuccessfully to generate satisfying partnerships with urban schools. It is not that schools cannot partner well. The best are experts at it. But many schools have a fixed staffing structure that does not allow for the capacity needed to recruit, train, and support strategic partnerships, much less individual volunteers. In addition, we lack robust models for tapping the diverse talents of volunteers. In-school volunteerism typically focuses on literacy and is typified by the adult (sitting in a much-too-small chair) reading with a child once a week in the back of a classroom. Community-based volunteering calls to mind coaching sports teams or mentoring a troubled teen. These are wonderful models of volunteer engagement, but they are far from sufficient. We need new models to tap the talents of adults from all walks of life. After-school programs can provide those models and leverage volunteer service to develop twenty-first century skills.

At Citizen Schools, we use after-school apprenticeship courses to engage thousands of adult volunteers each year. We invite them to teach what they know, what they do, and what they love—their vocations and their avocations—to middle school students. We call our volunteers "Citizen Teachers."

Each apprenticeship brings together two to four adults with ten to twelve children. Over the course of eleven weeks, the apprentices and their mentors team up to produce a product or performance designed to make adults say "WOW!" Apprenticeship WOWs! at Citizen Schools have included nine children's books that are now available at the Boston Public Library; solar cars that have competed successfully at a national competition at the Massachusetts Institute of Technology; PowerPoint presentations designed to teach senior citizens how to conduct genealogical research on the Web; a film, *If I Had a Minute with the President,* shown on national television; and architectural designs for a petting zoo proposed for the new Rose Kennedy Greenway, the park through downtown Boston made possible by the massive "Big Dig" highway project.

Apprenticeships are rigorous and relevant. Each of the projects described above required small teams to work with a leader to solve problems. The teams developed a high-quality presentation or product for an authentic audience through practice, feedback, and

NEW DIRECTIONS FOR YOUTH DEVELOPMENT • DOI: 10.1002/yd

revision and ultimately delivered a public presentation of their work.[22] Apprenticeships engage students as active learners and capable contributors to their communities. Natalie Pohlman, a designer at the prestigious Boston architectural firm Shepley Bullfinch Richardson and Abbott who led an apprenticeship noted, "The Citizen Schools apprentices worked really hard on their presentations. They learned that they have opinions about what works and what doesn't. They stop being passive spectators of the world around them."

One student's story

Sharnique Beck was an ambitious middle school student stuck in a low-performing school. Sharnique attended Citizen Schools for three years during middle school and took eight apprenticeship courses on topics including urban gardening, art, design, computer programming, and outdoor adventures. In her computer programming apprenticeship, Sharnique worked with Emily Leventhal, a young engineer who went on to study business at the Massachusetts Institute of Technology. Emily and Sharnique collaborated on a paper, "Mission Tetris: Teaching 8th Graders to Program Tetris." The paper was selected to be presented at the annual conference of the Society of Women Engineers. Sharnique, then age thirteen, traveled with Emily from Boston to Atlanta for the conference, where she presented her paper and attended presentations by women engineers. Sharnique, the youngest presenter at the conference, was extremely well received and found the experience inspirational. She now attends TechBoston, an alternative high school funded by the Gates Foundation, where she takes high-level computer programming and college preparatory classes. She hopes to attend MIT and pursue a career in computer programming.

Sharnique's story and the experience of thousands of Citizen Schools' apprenticeships demonstrate that after-school programs can engage adults from all walks of life and leverage their talents and commitment to develop twenty-first century skills. These programs can offer opportunities that are hard to come

NEW DIRECTIONS FOR YOUTH DEVELOPMENT • DOI: 10.1002/yd

by in the tightly structured school day: the chance to learn from an expert, apply that learning to a real-world challenge, and in doing so forge a connection with an adult who can bring more resources and more opportunities to the table (see Chapter 14, this volume).

Charting a new course for the after-school sector

America has much to gain from a strong after-school sector. Students will gain twenty-first century skills, experiences of mastery, and expanded college and career opportunities. Parents will be confident that their children are not only safe but also growing and learning during the after-school hours. Schools will have more competent, more motivated, and more complete students. Corporations will be able to hire workers who have the skills they need for the modern economy. Communities will have citizens of all ages who are connected to each other and know how to solve problems together.

With so much to gain, our field remains frustratingly far from fulfilling its promise. The after-school sector has not yet articulated a compelling value proposition, and it has not yet delivered compelling, large-scale results.

Today's after-school sector is still sorting out its identity. The field's rapid expansion began in the 1960s and 1970s when women entered the workforce in dramatic numbers. In 1960, approximately one quarter of mothers with school-age children worked outside the home. We had a national after-school program, and it was called Mom. Today the numbers are reversed, with three quarters of mothers of school-age children working outside the home. In many respects, the design and public perception of after-school programs still reflect the culture of child care. Programs offer supervised activities, such as arts and crafts, and provide a reliable bridge for parents from school dismissal until pick-up time after work.

In the 1980s, the child care paradigm was complemented by a public safety imperative. Amid a rising tide of juvenile crime and public perceptions of "super-predator" youth, after-school programs became the safe spaces that families and communities sought to keep kids off the streets. A decade or so later as the surging crime rate subsided, a new current swept into afterschool: the standards movement in education. As schools struggled to meet ever more stringent standards for student achievement, the after-school hours became a target for providing academic remediation. Programs were pushed to align their activities with in-school curricula. Attention shifted to homework completion and test preparation, and sometimes to mind-numbing drill and practice.

As a result of these shifting tides, today's after-school sector is riven by doubt and disagreement about its purpose. Is it a child care provider, a public safety strategy, a homework tutor, or some combination of these? Should its staff be trained, supervised, and perhaps accredited as child care workers, youth workers, or teachers? While it is not essential that all after-school programs aspire to identical goals or offer the same activities, this identity crisis is an obstacle to quality, investment, talent development, and public support. If people do not know what after-school programs are or are striving to become, they cannot establish high expectations and look for results.

The after-school sector can resolve its identity crisis in part by building on the platform and lessons learned from its recent past, but primarily by choosing a new path. A revitalized after-school sector will make twenty-first century skills its organizing principle and use that focus to engage students and the community, and deliver unmistakable results.

The sector also needs to invest in its future workforce. Current programs are beset by high turnover and low pay. There is no professional pathway for career development, training, credentialing, or advancement. If after-school programs are to fulfill their promise, they need to recruit and retain outstanding educators, community builders, and social entrepreneurs.

The best strategy for bringing great people to the field is to give them a chance to do great work. If after-school programs are crackling with creativity and a zest for learning, dynamic educators will want to be a part of them. Embracing a focus on twenty-first century skills and a program design of authentic, hands-on learning is a good first step. But more steps are needed.

One promising strategy is to partner with schools to hire educators who bridge the dismissal bell. This approach helps to ensure alignment between in-school and after-school learning and culture, an important and challenging objective that has been researched and well described by Biancarosa, Dechausay, and Noam in their book *Afterschool Education: Approaches to an Emerging Field.*[23]

The Edge, a program in Maine, has adopted a staffing strategy in partnership with its host school (after-school staff work a noon to 8:00 P.M. day, bridging school, afterschool, and home) and reports that it helps establish a level of professionalism and collegiality that is important for recruiting and retaining effective educators (C. Harrington, personal communication, January 2006). An additional strategy is to hire staff to link after-school programs with museums, libraries, and other education and youth development organizations. Combining a morning assignment at a museum, library, or school with an afternoon assignment in an after-school program can create a rewarding, full-time professional job. This is the approach we have taken at Citizen Schools with our Teaching Fellowship program. In the morning, teaching fellows work with our partner schools or nonprofits, typically helping them expand and improve their curricula and youth outreach efforts. For example, one teaching fellow works at the Boston Public Library developing hands-on activities for a special collection of historic maps. What started as a staffing strategy has evolved into a broader initiative to professionalize the after-school workforce. Now our teaching fellows also enroll in a fully accredited master's degree program that Citizen Schools created with Lesley University.

Perhaps most important, the after-school sector needs to invest in quality and deliver compelling results.[24] Recent national evaluations have reported that many federally funded after-school programs fail to engage students and do little to drive gains in achievement. While after-school advocates have challenged the methodology of these studies, and with valid arguments, the studies' core criticism remains piercing. One consequence of mediocrity is that the after-school sector has failed to attract a broad social commitment or financial investment commensurate with its potential. Underinvestment only perpetuates mediocrity. After-school practitioners need to accept this candid critique and respond to it with vigor and rigor. But how?

The after-school field is extremely decentralized, with most programs operating at only one site and serving only a few dozen students. The after-school sector needs to nurture national market leaders who will set and raise performance standards. These national organizations will convey credibility, attract talented staff, engage the private sector, build infrastructure, and test new approaches to evaluation. There will still be plenty of room for local initiatives and single-site providers; national organizations will meet only a small portion of the total demand. But as in many private sector industries, recognized "brands" will help to create, define, and organize the market. They will establish consumer expectations and patterns of practice that are essential for a market to develop and mature.

With a clearer focus on teaching twenty-first century skills, robust hands-on learning activities, and a talented pool of teachers and leaders, strong after-school programs can deliver strong results. In a more mature market, strong programs will prosper and attract investment, while programs that lag their peers will attract less interest from parents, students, schools, and community partners. This process will be neither smooth nor easy, but it is essential if the after-school field is to earn its place as a full and valued partner with parents and schools in teaching our nation's children.

After-school programs can teach twenty-first century skills, and they can do much more. They can become the leading edge of authentic education reform. They can build social capital, forge connections between youth and adults, and reinvigorate the lives of communities. They can help individuals aspire to their dreams and help our nation achieve its highest ideals.

Notes

1. James-Burdumy, S., Dynarski, M., Moore, M., Deke, J., Mansfield, W., and Pistorino, C. (2005, May 5). *When schools stay open late: The national evaluation of the twenty-first century Community Learning Centers Program: Final*

report. Washington, DC: U.S. Department of Education, National Center for Education Evaluation and Regional Assistance. http://www.ed.gov/ies/ncee.

2. Levy, F., & Murnane, R. J. (2004, April 29). *Preparing students to thrive in twenty-first century America: The role for after-school.* Paper presented at Reimagining After-School Conference, Washington, DC.

3. Pink, D. H. (2005, June 4). Pomp and circumspect. *New York Times,* p. 29.

4. National Commission on Excellence in Education. (1983, April). *A Nation at Risk: The Imperative for Educational Reform.* A Report to the Nation and the Secretary of Education, United States Department of Education. Washington, DC: U.S. Government Printing Office.

5. National Assessment of Educational Progress. (2002). *The nation's report card.* Washington, DC: Author. http://www.nces.ed.gov/nationsreportcard.

6. Campbell, J. R., Voelkl, K. E., and Donahue, P. L. (1996). *NAEP 1996 trends in academic progress.* Washington, DC: U.S. Department of Education, National Center for Education Statistics.

7. Dillon, S. (2005, December 26). Literacy falls for graduates from college, testing finds. *New York Times,* p. 1.

8. Levy, F., & Murnane, R. J. (1997). *Teaching the new basic skills.* New York: Simon & Schuster.

9. Gardner, H. (1991). *The unschooled mind.* New York: Basic Books.

10. Programme for International Student Assessment. (2003). *Problem solving for tomorrow's world: First measures of cross-curricular competencies from PISA 2003.* http://pisa.oced.org/document/54.

11. Cohen, D. K. (1988). Teaching practice: Plus ça change. In P. W. Jackson (Ed.), *Contributing to educational change.* Berkeley: McCutchan. Ablelmann, C., & Elmore, R. (1999). *When accountability knocks, will anyone answer?* www.cpre.org/Publications/rr42.pdf.

12. National Foundation for Teaching Entrepreneurship. (2005). http://www.nfte.com/whatwedo.

13. National Foundation for Teaching Entrepreneurship. (2005).

14. John Dewey is the patron saint of project-based learning, and it could be argued that he got his start in an after-school program. In the 1890s, when Dewey was chairing the School of Education at the University of Chicago, he became a close friend of Jane Addams, who had just opened Hull-House, a settlement house serving immigrant families in Chicago's Nineteenth Ward. Dewey had a close association with Hull-House and it was there, amid after-school clubs, drama and choral societies, and skill-building classes, that he began to develop his progressive educational philosophy focusing on the marriage of knowledge and experience. Dewey sought to activate the inner motivations of the learner by embedding learning in real-world tasks like cooking and carpentry. Schwarz, E. (2004, Spring). "After school time." *Lesley University Alumni Magazine.*

15. Levy, F., and Murnane, R. J. (2004, April 29). *Preparing students to thrive in twenty-first century America: The role for after-school.* Paper presented at the Reimagining After-School Conference, Washington, DC.

16. Resnick, L. B. (1987) "Learning in school and out." *Educational Researcher, 16*(9), 13–20.

17. Brown, J. S., Collins, A., & Holum, A. (1991). Cognitive apprenticeship: Making thinking visible. *American Educator, 15*(3), 6–11, 38–46.

18. Levy & Murnane. (1997).

19. Levy & Murnane. (1997).

20. Vander Ark, M. (2006, January). Presented at High Schools of the Future: Lessons for Reforming schools, Worcester, MA.

21. Conversations with many volunteer Citizen Teachers and their employers led us to believe that the apprenticeship model helps to build new workforce skills among the volunteers as well as the students.

22. Schelgel, C. (2003). *Bridging difference: Interaction and learning through civic work.* Unpublished doctoral dissertation, Harvard University.

23. Biancarosa, G., Dechausay, N., & Noam, G. (2003). *Afterschool education: Approaches to an emerging field.* Cambridge, MA: Harvard Education Press.

24. While some national evaluations have cast doubt on the potential for after-school programs to advance achievement, rigorous evaluations of some programs indicate there are powerful models that can deliver results. For example, an external evaluation by Policy Studies Associates (PSA) is validating that the Citizen Schools approach works. Phase III of a seven-year comparison-group evaluation concludes that Citizen Schools has been successful at building public speaking skills, academic success, and the ability to work well with adults. In particular, students scored better than a matched comparison group on the Seventh Grade English Language Arts MCAS assessment, which includes a persuasive essay, and the Eighth Grade Math MCAS assessment, which includes higher-level problem solving, word problems, and short-answer questions. "Early evidence suggests that Citizen Schools has had a positive impact on the short-term outcomes that it seeks for its participants," concluded PSA, "and in doing so, has moved a group of low-income and educationally at-risk participants toward a trajectory of successful high school completion and advancement on to college." Espino, J., Fabiano, L., and Pearson, L. (2004, July 1). "Citizen Schools: Evidence from two student cohorts on the use of community resources to promote youth development—Phase II report of the Citizen Schools evaluation." Washington, DC: Policy Studies Associates.www.policystudies.com/studies/youth/CS9.20 Report_pdf.

ERIC SCHWARZ *is president and CEO of Citizen Schools, a leading national education initiative that helps improve student achievement by blending real-world learning and rigorous academics after school.*

DAVID STOLOW *is director of strategic development for Citizen Schools.*

NEW DIRECTIONS FOR YOUTH DEVELOPMENT • DOI: 10.1002/yd

New Technology High School is an exemplary twenty-first century learning school, employing project- and problem-based learning and outcomes-based assessment.

8

Twenty-first century learning in schools: A case study of New Technology High School in Napa, California

Bob Pearlman

WE HAVE KNOWN for years what students need to know and be able to do in the twenty-first century. Starting with the Secretary's Commission on Achieving Necessary Skills (SCANS) report from the U.S. Department of Labor, *What Work Requires of Schools*, in 1991,[1] it was clear that twenty-first century learning was to be built on a foundation of basic knowledge, but went well beyond basics to include a significant set of twenty-first century skills.

SCANS anticipated the profound changes coming in the 1990s, including globalization and the increased role of technology in work and life. It was the first significant report that argued that students would need to be smarter and also better communicators, collaborators, and performers for the workplace and society of the future. SCANS said that future workplace know-how requires thinking skills, personal qualities (responsibility, self-management),

WILEY
InterScience®
DISCOVER SOMETHING GREAT

NEW DIRECTIONS FOR YOUTH DEVELOPMENT, NO. 110, SUMMER 2006 © WILEY PERIODICALS, INC.
Published online in Wiley InterScience (www.interscience.wiley.com) • DOI: 10.1002/yd.170

project management, interpersonal skills (teamwork, leadership), information skills, systems skills, and technology utilization skills.

In *Learning for the Twenty-First Century*, the Partnership for 21st Century Skills updated and enhanced SCANS.[2] *Learning* again builds on core subjects, but shows that twenty-first century learning includes information and communication skills, thinking and problem-solving skills, interpersonal and self-directional skills, and the skills to use twenty-first century tools such as information and communication technologies. But what sets *Learning* apart from all previous studies is its finding that assessment and feedback to students is the key to skill mastery.

In the United States and other countries, particularly Europe and Asia, leaders are grappling with designing schools that serve the needs of the twenty-first century. In Singapore, where the national slogan is "Thinking Schools, Learning Nation," Tharman Shanmugaratnam, the minister of state for trade, industry, and education, says that "one of the key adjustments under way is in the way we educate our young so as to develop in them a willingness to keep learning, and an ability to experiment, innovate, and take risks. Our ability to create and innovate will be Singapore's most important asset in [the] future."[3]

In the United Kingdom, the national government's $80 billion Building Schools for the Future program aims to rebuild every secondary school in the country over a ten- to fifteen-year period. Its mission is "Working together to create world-class, twenty-first-century schools—environments which will inspire learning for decades to come and provide exceptional assets for the whole community."

So while we and others have a good picture of what students need to learn and be able to do, key questions remain. How do they learn it? How do students know they know it? And what do schools look like where twenty-first century learning takes place?

Designing twenty-first century schools and learning starts with asking what knowledge and skills students need for the twenty-first century. But real design needs to go much further and address these questions:

NEW DIRECTIONS FOR YOUTH DEVELOPMENT • DOI: 10.1002/yd

- What learning curricula, activities, and experiences foster twenty-first century learning?
- What assessments for learning, school based and national, foster student learning, engagement, and self-direction?
- What physical learning environments (classroom, school, and real world) foster twenty-first century student learning?
- How can technology support a twenty-first century collaborative learning environment and support a learning community?

The key design issues might be illustrated this way:

Knowledge and Skills → Curricula → Assessments → Facilities→ Technology

Every country has done a good job of articulating the knowledge and skills that students need, but few have developed or identified the curricula, assessments, facilities, and technology that would foster twenty-first century learning.

New Technology High School: A case study of a twenty-first century school

Walk into a classroom at New Technology High School (NTHS) in Napa, California, and you will see students at work: writing journals online, doing research on the Internet, meeting in groups to plan and make their Web sites and their digital media presentations, and evaluating their peers for collaboration and presentation skills. Another teacher's students may also be there in a team-taught interdisciplinary course. These activities have a name and a purpose. This is project-based learning, and it is designed to engage students in learning deeply.

Despite its name, NTHS is not a technology school, although there is more technology at the school than most others. NTHS was founded in 1996 as a twenty-first century school. A task force led by the business community but including educators and civic leaders studied best practices throughout the United States and launched a school with that aim.

In its first years, NTHS teachers defined the school's eight learning outcomes: content standards, collaboration, critical thinking, oral communication, written communication, career preparation, citizenship and ethics, and technology literacy. These outcomes map to the SCANS standards, which inspired them, and also to more recent articulations of twenty-first century skills. The New Tech teachers designed them not to be a wall poster or a compendium no one looks at. Instead, NTHS embeds these learning outcomes in all projects, assessments, and grade reports.

Students graduate from NTHS demonstrating mastery of the eight learning outcomes through a digital portfolio. The portfolio, which New Tech calls a professional portfolio, is a public online document that is alive on the NTHS Web site throughout the student's career at the school. It is a work-in-progress until the end of the senior year, when it is submitted for graduation.

Project- and problem-based learning: Keys to twenty-first century learning

"We needed a new type of instruction that better reflected the goals we wanted each student to achieve, demonstrate, and document," says Paul Curtis, one of the original lead teachers at NTHS and now director of curriculum for the New Technology Foundation. NTHS teachers start each unit with a realistic or real-world project that both engages interest and generates a list of things the students need to know. Projects are designed to tackle complex problems, requiring critical thinking. NTHS's strategy is simple:

- To learn collaboration, work in teams.
- To learn critical thinking, take on complex problems.
- To learn oral communication, present.
- To learn written communication, write.
- To learn technology, use technology.
- To develop citizenship, take on civic and global issues.

- To learn about careers, do internships.
- To learn content, research and do all of the above.

This strategy can be built into the curriculum if students work on projects that are designed to elicit collaboration, critical thinking, written communication, oral communication, work ethic, and other critical skills while simultaneously meeting state or national content standards.

In traditional classrooms students typically work alone, work on short, noncomplex assignments that emphasize short-term content memorization, write for the teacher alone, and rarely make presentations. Project- and problem-based learning takes a different approach:

1. Put students into teams of three or more students, who work on an in-depth project for three to eight weeks.
2. Start the project by introducing a complex entry question, and scaffold the project with activities and new information that deepens the work.
3. Develop a time line for the project through plans, drafts, timely benchmarks, and presentations by the team to an outside panel of experts drawn from parents and the community.
4. Provide timely assessments to students on their projects for content, oral communication, written communication, teamwork, critical thinking, and other critical skills.

At NTHS some examples of projects include presenting a plan to Congress on solving the oil crisis, addressing economic issues as a team of the president's economic advisers, or inventing, under contract from the National Aeronautics and Space Administration, new sports that astronauts can play on the moon so they can get exercise.

Calendaring, that is, providing a time line, is crucial. Few students, or adults, can work effectively without a clear timetable and benchmarks. At NTHS, the calendar for each project, called the course agenda, is available online and linked to the project briefcase, which holds all the project resources, calendar, and assessment rubrics. The project briefcase organizes all project materials for student access, action, and project management.

Project-based learning is often confused with projects, which are short activities injected into traditional education to liven things as a culminating event for the unit. Real project-based learning, by contrast, is deep, complex, and rigorous.

Many countries have had difficulties with project-based learning in the past, when curricula were not designed effectively and scaffolded to ensure that essential learning takes place. In Queensland, Australia, a new, major provincewide initiative in project-based learning is called "Rich Tasks." In 2005, fifty-six schools in Queensland offered programs from Year 1 to Year 9 based on the New Basics triad, which emphasizes what is taught (New Basics), how it is taught (Pedagogy), and how kids show they have learned it (Rich Tasks) (http://education.qld.gov.au/corporate/newbasics). In the United Kingdom, Homewood School in Kent calls it "Total Learning." Starting in 2005, Homewood revamped its year 7 and year 8 programs into a project-based, integrated thematic curriculum. Students at NTHS learn and master collaboration skills, a key twenty-first century skill, by working in project teams, with one student taking on the role of project manager. The team develops a contract outlining the scope of work for each student member. Projects culminate with team reports and presentations. After the completion of the project, each member of the team evaluates the other members through a peer collaboration rubric. At NTHS all teams have taken on a rule that a student who slacks can be voted off the team. The penalty is that the student must then do the whole project alone.

Assessment for twenty-first century learning

In a recent *Education Week* Commentary, Tony Wagner described a rubric that principals in Hawaii had developed to assess rigor in the classroom. The principals, Wagner writes, "began to realize that rigor has less to do with how demanding the material the teacher covers is than with what competencies students have mastered as a result of a lesson."[4] The group determined to define the level of rigor by posing these questions to students: Why is this important to learn? In what ways am I challenged to think in this lesson? How will I apply, assess, or communicate what I have learned? How will I know how good my work is and how I can improve it?

Project- and problem-based learning does not work unless a learner gets feedback to "know how good my work is and how I can improve it." Current assessments do not do the job. State testing and accountability is aimed at schools, not individual student learning, and reports only once a year, after students have moved on to other teachers. Periodic assessments in managed curriculums are done once a month and mainly provide information to teachers. A student cannot get better or become the manager of his or her own learning without constant, real-time assessment and feedback. This is called assessment for learning, as opposed to assessment for school, district, or classroom accountability.

Assessment for learning starts with outcomes; proceeds with projects, products, and performances that map to the outcomes; and completes the loop with assessment and feedback to students:

Outcomes → Projects → Product and Performance → Assessment/Feedback

Most schools give students a single grade for a course, often losing important data about the skills and abilities of the students. At NTHS, student course grades are disaggregated into the component "learning outcomes." Instead of a single composite grade for each project, subject, or integrated course, the grade report for a project or a course shows separate and distinct grades for content, critical thinking, written communication, oral communication, technology literacy, and any of the other learning outcomes appropriate for the course. Students get a report card that reflects how well they are performing on twenty-first century knowledge and skills. In that way, they know exactly where they are performing well and where they are not.

At NTHS the gradebook is online, accessible by password, and "living": it is updated whenever there is new information, not just at the end of term. Students are thus constantly aware of their strengths and weaknesses and can target their efforts toward improvement. This continuous and just-in-time feedback is critical in supplying the information that helps students become self-directed learners. The assessment for learning feedback is also available online in real time to teachers and parents, who can also easily identify student strengths and weaknesses and offer support to students.

NTHS has developed unique ways to assess certain twenty-first century skills. At the end of every project, students assess every member of their project team using an online peer collaboration rubric. Scores go to a database, where a student, through a secure password, can see his or her scores, although the evaluations are anonymous. The student can then publish these scores as evidence for his or her digital portfolio. A similar process is followed with an online presentation evaluation rubric, which is scored by teachers and visiting community experts.

Schools as workplaces for twenty-first century students

If students are to be the workers, they need classroom learning environments that are workplaces for both individual and group work and are equipped with the technology and tools they need to do their work. Traditional school classrooms are typically 750 to 1,000 square feet for thirty or more students, providing an environment suited only to teacher-led instruction, particularly at the secondary school level.

Larger classrooms are needed that provide a students-at-work environment involving computers, group work, planning, presentations, team teaching, and other strategies. NTHS accomplishes this through double-size classrooms, 1,400 to 1,800 square feet, that house up to fifty students and two teachers in a team-taught interdisciplinary course. The room is divided into two general sections, either side-by-side or exterior ring to interior center. One section houses desktop or laptop computers, one per student, wired or wireless (or both), for individual or small team work; the other section houses flexible tables for small group work and planning, and doubles as a space for student presentations and teacher-led planning activities or teacher lectures. Teacher lectures are rare but are delivered on what NTHS calls a "need-to-know" basis: when students express a need to understand concepts and content critical to their project work.

NTHS looks more like a modern high-tech office than a school. When one walks through NTHS's glass-walled corridors, one sees students at work. Enrollment is four hundred students for grades 9 to 12. The smaller size helps to establish a more personal environment and a culture suited for individual and group work.

Technology and the twenty-first century classroom

Technology plays a critical role in supporting twenty-first century learning environments. Providing one-to-one computing gives students and teachers the hardware and software tools to do their work. But even more profound, technology, through the school's network, provides a collaborative learning environment that houses curriculum, assessment rubrics, living gradebooks, and communication tools.

Many schools and states around the world are experimenting with one-to-one computing for students and finding the results lacking. The reason for these results is that they use a traditional curricular approach that fails to engage students as directors of their own learning. Project- and problem-based learning, by contrast, can bring one-to-one computing to life.

By having their own computer and Internet access, students at NTHS can research any topic, communicate with experts and teachers, write journals and reports, develop presentations through PowerPoint and video, and take responsibility to develop their professional digital portfolio demonstrating evidence of their mastery of the school's twenty-first century learning outcomes.

In theory, technology is not needed for project-based learning. However, it enables students to research, plan, and communicate.

NEW DIRECTIONS FOR YOUTH DEVELOPMENT • DOI: 10.1002/yd

Moreover, NTHS goes beyond one-to-one computing and provides a technology platform that serves as a collaborative learning environment for students and teachers. This environment, the New Tech High Learning System, comprises the curriculum, standards, assessment tools, and reporting tools of New Technology High School, all online on a common IBM Lotus Notes technology platform.

The learning system is an enterprise solution for the whole school. For students, it is the medium through which they work and learn. It enables them to self-manage their work, collaborate with others, and see their assessments and grades daily. All projects include a course agenda or calendar, where teachers enter deadlines as well as activities for each day, including links to resources and daily assignments.

The learning system also immediately and dynamically publishes all the project materials to the Web for access to the curriculum anywhere, anytime, by students and their parents. And because all projects are housed online, they are available year-to-year even if teachers leave. Moreover, the projects can be shared by teachers within a school and between schools. Currently there are fourteen schools nationally that are based on the New Technology High School model and sharing projects. The network schools will increase to twenty-eight in 2006.

Twenty-first century learners

NTHS is a different kind of school and it produces a different kind of student. Students report feeling safer, better known, challenged, more engaged, and more motivated for postsecondary learning. A study that surveyed the school's eight graduation classes strongly suggests that students feel New Tech High's use of project-based learning and focus on twenty-first century skills were important in preparing them for college, careers, and citizenship.[5] Ninety-eight percent of NTHS's seniors report postsecondary enrollment plans, compared to 67 percent that the Napa Valley Unified School District reports. California and the United States graduate 67 percent and 71 percent of high school students, respectively, of which 32 percent in California and 34 percent nationally are deemed college ready.

Furthermore, the alumni study found that 40 percent of all NTHS graduates and 37 percent of graduating girls either pursue college study, complete college study, or work in science, technology, engineering, or math careers, compared to 7 percent nationally. Women today constitute 45 percent of the workforce in the United States, but hold just 12 percent of science and engineering jobs in business and industry.

NTHS's twenty-first century learners are articulate, powerful, and self-directed collaborators and entrepreneurs.

The globalization challenge

Globalization is flattening the world and challenging the United States as never before, as Tom Friedman points out in *The World Is Flat.*[6] Students in the United States and other advanced countries must lead a new era of global cooperation as twenty-first century learners. Societies need citizens who are smarter, more creative, and more capable of leading, managing, collaborating, and networking with productive people around the world.

Schools need to be totally redesigned to enable and facilitate twenty-first century learning. New Technology High School is one way of getting there. Countries need to upgrade their educational standards to world-class standards, moving curriculum to 100 percent in-depth project- and problem-based learning that involves teamwork, critical thinking, and communication skills; authentically assessing for learning all these skills for immediate and active feedback to students; redesigning and reconstructing facilities and classrooms to enable a students-at-work environment for individual and collaborative work; and finally, using technology to bind this collaborative learning community together.

Notes

1. U.S. Department of Labor (1991). What work requires of schools: A SCANS report for America 2000. Secretary's Commission on Achieving Necessary Skills. http://wdr.doleta.gov/SCANS/whatwork.

2. Partnership for 21st Century Skills. (2003). *Learning for the twenty-first century: A report and MILE Guide for twenty-first century skills.* Washington, DC: Author. http://www.21stcenturyskills.org/images/stories/otherdocs/P21_Report.pdf.

3. Borja, R. R. (2004, May 6). Technology counts 2004. *Education Week.* 2004. http://counts.edweek.org/sreports/tc04/article.cfm?slug=35singapore.h23.

4. Wagner, T. (2006, January 11). Rigor on trial. *Education Week.*

5. Rockman *et al.* (2006). New Technology High School postsecondary student success story. http://www.newtechfoundation.org/Articles/NTF_StudentSuccessStudy.pdf.

6. Friedman, T. L. (2005). *The world is flat: A brief history of the twenty-first century.* New York: Farrar, Straus and Giroux.

BOB PEARLMAN *is director of strategic planning for the New Technology Foundation and a consultant on designing twenty-first century secondary schools. The New Technology Foundation supports the replication of the New Technology High School model in twenty-four sites across the United States.*

Indianapolis's school district is pioneering a systemic approach to twenty-first century learning with digital age teacher training and the use of data and technology.

9

Twenty-first century learning in school systems: The case of the Metropolitan School District of Lawrence Township, Indianapolis, Indiana

Marcia Capuano, Troy Knoderer

IN NOVEMBER 2000, the Lilly Endowment of Indianapolis, Indiana, issued a request for grant proposals from public school districts in Marion County, Indiana. It called for school districts to develop innovative, systemic, and transforming approaches to preparing students to thrive in an increasingly competitive, high-tech, global society. The Metropolitan School District of Lawrence Township's (MSDLT) response was a $5.9 million dollar request to launch the Digital Age Literacy Initiative.

The MSDLT is a large Indianapolis school district, urban and suburban, serving more than sixteen thousand students and employing more than a thousand teachers. Rich in diversity, Lawrence Township students reflect the following demographic makeup:

NEW DIRECTIONS FOR YOUTH DEVELOPMENT, NO. 110, SUMMER 2006 © WILEY PERIODICALS, INC.
Published online in Wiley InterScience (www.interscience.wiley.com) • DOI: 10.1002/yd.171

113

- White: 50.6 percent
- Black: 35.1 percent
- Hispanic: 7.0 percent
- Multiracial: 5.5 percent
- Asian: 1.7 percent
- American Indian: 0.1 percent

The MSD mission, according to its mission statement, "is to empower all students with the knowledge and skills, compassion and integrity needed to contribute and succeed as self-directed, life-long learners in a competitive global community." Through the work of the Digital Age Literacy Initiative, MSDLT has developed and implemented the body of knowledge and the twenty-first century skills necessary for students to succeed as self-directed learners in the digital age. The three paradigm-shifting goals of the initiative provide the content, process, and context to both enliven and meet the district's mission statement:

Content: Broaden the scope of literacy to include digital age skills.
Process: Implement a systemic professional development framework.
Context: Reinvent the district as a professional learning community.

Today's students are growing up in a digital age. In a world of abundant, interactive, multimedia information, paper-and-pencil literacy is no longer adequate for students, who are projected to have as many as nine different careers during their working lives. In addition to strong reading and writing skills, they will need to be literate in many other areas to thrive in a global, knowledge-driven world. LT is empowering students with the following digital age literacies and twenty-first century skills, adapted from the research of the North Central Regional Educational Laboratory (NCREL) and the Metiri Group:

- *Basic literacy:* Language and numeracy proficiency using conventional or technology-based media

- *Technological literacy:* Competence in the use of computers, networks, applications, and other technological devices
- *Visual literacy:* The ability to decipher, interpret, and express ideas using images, graphics, icons, charts, graphs, and video
- *Information literacy:* The competence to find, evaluate, and make use of information appropriately
- *Global awareness/cultural competence:* The ability and willingness to form authentic relationships across differences
- *Self-direction:* The ability to set goals, plan for achievement, independently manage time and effort, and independently assess the quality of one's learning and any products that result
- *Higher-order thinking/sound reasoning:* Process of analysis, comparison, inference and interpretation, synthesis, and evaluation

Before students can learn those skills, their teachers must master the skills themselves. Research confirms that high-quality, systemic, and ongoing professional development for teachers is the most effective way to improve student learning.[1] Coaching is the best professional development method for ensuring that teachers apply new strategies.[2] Consequently, Lawrence Township has trained thirty-four master teachers to serve as digital age literacy coaches who facilitate teachers' implementation of digital age skills and the ongoing self-reflection on their own teaching practices. Each elementary school has one coach, and each middle school and high school has up to three coaches each.

The digital age literacy coaches serve as the primary vehicle to assist teachers and principals in the understanding and classroom application of twenty-first century skills. Within the school day, these instructional coaches provide teachers the following types of job-embedded opportunities to learn and practice twenty-first century skills:

- Workshops
- Study groups
- Action research

- Book studies
- Model teaching
- Coteaching
- Individual coaching and consulting

One of the primary goals of the coaching relationship is to encourage teachers to become self-reflective about their teaching. Using professional development tools like action research and cognitive coaching, the instructional coaches help the teachers develop the necessary skills to self-analyze, self-reflect, and make subsequent modifications to their teaching. Through the process of action research, Lawrence teachers self-evaluate the integration of the twenty-first century skills into their teaching.

The role of the building and district-level administrator has been just as critical in the systemic implementation of twenty-first century learning. Every building principal has been trained in the twenty-first century skills as well as other areas of instructional leadership.

Evidence of progress

For teachers to truly integrate the twenty-first century skills into their classroom instruction, assessments to measure student growth in those skills must be available. To that end, the district's digital age literacy coaches and representative teachers partnered with the Metiri Group of California in the development of a variety of assessments, including classroom and district-level online inventories and twenty-first century skill rubrics.

As coaches facilitate action research with classroom teachers, the Self-Directed Learning Inventory developed in partnership with the Metiri Group allows teachers to measure student growth in self-direction. For instance, Figure 9.1 shows the inventory results for a group of high school students in four specific areas of self-direction. As part of the action research process, the high school English teacher and coach were measuring the results of five

Figure 9.1. Results of five instructional strategies aimed at improving students' self-direction

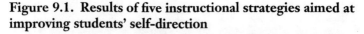
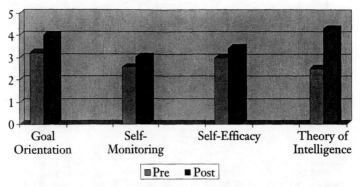

Key: 5 = very true of me; 4 = true of me; 3 = kind of true of me; 2 = only a little true of me; 1 = not at all true of me

Note: This self-reporting assessment aggregates student answers to a series of questions for each category (goal orientation, self-monitoring, and so forth). The numerical response equivalents are then averaged to assign a score for each category of self-direction. The pre/post refers to the instructional strategies implemented in an attempt to influence self-direction. The "pre" column reflects the average score prior to any instructional intervention. The "post" represents the average score for students after the learning experience.

instructional strategies aimed at improving students' self-direction before and after the strategies were used.

Lawrence Township teachers may also build rubrics that integrate the skills of twenty-first century learning with state standards by using the online rubric maker housed within the district's professional development Web site. From the district-level rubrics for twenty-first century skill areas, teachers may choose individual skills to measure that fit the particular student work or process being addressed. For example, one second-grade teacher needed to measure student performance in three areas of self-direction and one area of visual literacy (Table 9.1). In addition, she chose to integrate additional skills that applied to the student performance. Lawrence Township also uses district-wide inventories as summative measurements of the system's growth.

The Mankato Survey offers a self-assessment tool for both students and teachers related to practical classroom access, ability, and use of technology. The instrument assesses access to technology at

Table 9.1. Measuring areas of self-direction, second grade

Skill	Emerging (1)	Developing (2)	Proficient (3)	Exemplary (4)
Twenty-First Century Learning (Self-Direction)				
Planning	Student shows no evidence of planning strategies.	Teacher guides student through the development of a plan.	Teacher provides occasional assistance in choosing planning strategies.	Student independently chooses planning strategies
Focused on task	Student is unfocused and not on task.	Teacher provides frequent redirection.	Teacher provides occasional redirection.	Student is independently engaged during the assigned task.
Self-monitoring	Student does not self-monitor.	Student self-monitors with teacher guidance.	Student needs occasional redirection from teacher to self-monitor.	Student independently self-monitors.
State Standards				
Visual literacy	Pictures do not match words.	Few pictures and words match.	Pictures occasionally match words.	Pictures completely match words.
Flow chart components	Includes none of the components.	Includes one of three components.	Includes two of three components.	Includes title, arrows, and appropriate colors.
Mechanics	There are more than four errors in capitalization, punctuation, or grammar.	There are four errors in grammar, capitalization, or punctuation.	There are two to three errors in grammar, punctuation, or capitalization.	There are zero to one errors in grammar, punctuation, or capitalization.

school and at home: uses of basic word processing, file management, spreadsheets, databases, graphics, Internet, research, e-mail, and technology presentations.

In 2001, a random sample of MSDLT fifth-, eighth-, and twelfth-grade teachers and students completed the Mankato Survey. The analysis compared students and teachers' perspectives of technology access, ability, and use. The survey has assisted MSDLT in determining the overall levels of technology competency for students and staff, as part of formulating the district's long-range technology plan. Professional development staff have used the baseline survey results to design professional development opportunities for educators and to plan meaningful technology-rich lessons for students. In spring 2004, the district administered the Mankato Survey for the second time. Because different students were surveyed in each administration, changes in scores reflect changes in the system, not changes in individual students. The overall conclusions were that there were significant gains in spreadsheet use, research, and information searching and technology presentation for all students (elementary, middle, and high school) and consistent significant gains in nearly all categories for middle and high school students. (See Figures 9.2, 9.3, and 9.4.)

Sustainability

To support this ongoing learning for teachers and students, the district is reinventing itself as a professional learning community. Both administrators and teachers participate in reflective and collaborative learning communities focused on shared mission, vision, and values; collective inquiry; collaborative teams; action orientation and experimentation; continuous improvement; and results orientation.[3] The district recognizes that functioning as a professional learning community is key to sustaining and institutionalizing the initial work of the Digital Age Literacy Initiative.

Throughout the initiative, the district has devoted resources to the development and facilitation of a professional development

NEW DIRECTIONS FOR YOUTH DEVELOPMENT • DOI: 10.1002/yd

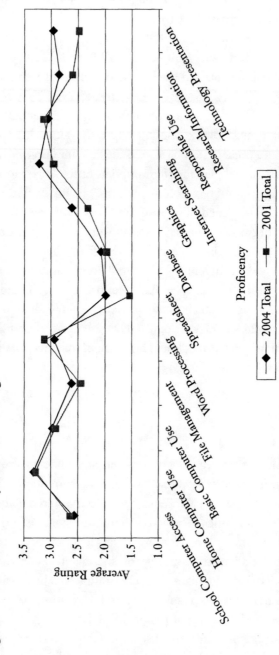

Figure 9.2. Mankato survey results for fifth graders, 2001 and 2005

Key: The instrument allows for four levels of response: 1 = no usage, implementation, or awareness; 2 = low level usage, implementation, or awareness; 3 = moderate level of usage, implementation, or awareness; 4 = highest level of usage, implementation, or awareness.

Administration of survey, 2000; survey results back, analysis, and action plan, 2001.

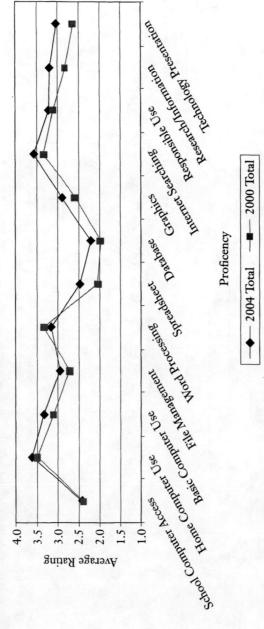

Figure 9.3. Mankato survey results for eighth graders, 2001 and 2005

Key: The instrument allows for four levels of response: 1 = no usage, implementation, or awareness; 2 = low level usage, implementation, or awareness; 3 = moderate level of usage, implementation, or awareness; 4 = highest level of usage, implementation, or awareness.

Administration of survey, 2000; survey results back, analysis, and action plan, 2001.

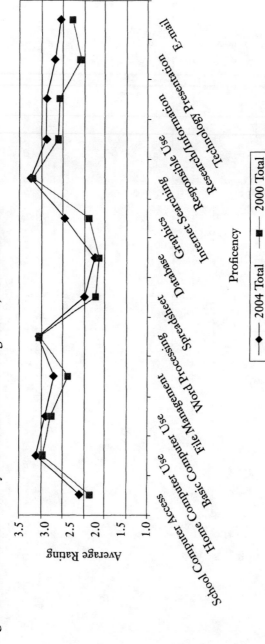

Figure 9.4. Mankato survey results for eleventh graders, 2001 and 2005

Legend: 2004 Total ◆ — 2000 Total ■

Proficency

Y-axis: Average Rating (1.0, 1.5, 2.0, 2.5, 3.0, 3.5)

X-axis categories: School Computer Access Use, Home Computer Use, Basic Computer Use, File Management, Worp Processing, Spreadsheet, Database, Graphics, Internet Searching, Responsible/Information Presentation, Research/Information, Technology, E-mail

Key: The instrument allows for four levels of response: 1 = no usage, implementation, or awareness; 2 = low level usage, implementation, or awareness; 3 = moderate level of usage, implementation, or awareness; 4 = highest level of usage, implementation, or awareness.

Administration of survey, 2000; survey results back, analysis, and action plan, 2001.

Web site. One of the primary goals of this site is to promote an online professional learning community.

Research suggests that teachers, like their students and other adults, are increasingly relying on "just-in-time" learning, through online courses and Internet-based knowledge.[4] To meet this need professionally, Lawrence Township built an online professional development network for its teachers. This online learning environment, the LT Online, is a critical component of the systemic professional development framework. By using this online network, Lawrence educators gain access to online courses, articles, rubric development, and professional conversations related to twenty-first century learning.

Many interactive online courses, some for graduate credit, have been offered in the following twenty-first century learning areas:

- Visual literacy
- Information literacy
- Self-direction
- Authentic learning
- Higher-order thinking
- Technological literacy
- Basic literacy: workshop approach
- Inquiry-based learning

For building and facilitating the professional development Web site, the district has relied primarily on the work of the thirty-four digital age literacy coaches. However, the district is currently piloting classroom teachers as facilitators for online experiences.

In addition, the role of the district's digital age advisory group has been instrumental in the development, growth, and sustainability of the professional development Web site. Through the Digital Age Literacy Advisory Group, the district seeks to integrate master teachers, administrators, parents, university faculty, and state and national digital age literacy experts into a professional learning community that will continue to guide the initiative. The district's partnership with the Metiri Group, Purdue University, and the Partnership for 21st Century Skills has significantly contributed to developing, implementing, and sustaining the Digital Age Literacy Initiative.

The members of the Digital Age Literacy Advisory Group provide external expertise to the district; however, the district has also made additional significant efforts to cultivate sustainable internal expertise by developing teacher leaders. Not only have teachers from each building in the district developed and implemented twenty-first century learning rubrics, they have also been trained to provide leadership in the area of cultural competence. Although the model of professional development will look different when the coaches return to the classroom in the 2007–2008 school year, the district is certain that through the work of the building administrator and teacher leaders, professional growth will occur around twenty-first century learning.

Conclusion

The cutting-edge quality of this Digital Age Literacy Initiative has implications beyond Lawrence Township as well. In an initial letter of support for the initiative, Cheryl Lemke, the Metiri Group consultant to the initiative, wrote that the work of MSDLT within the Digital Age Literacy Initiative "will serve as a test bed for the nation . . . [and] has the potential to change the face of American education—providing leadership in redefining literacy for the digital age." Now, four years into the initiative, Lemke reflects on the contributions of Lawrence Township within the national context of twenty-first century learning:

As a pioneer in this new movement toward twenty-first century learning, [Lawrence Township has] contributed greatly to the field's understanding of how such skills can be embedded in everyday teaching and learning. In particular, [Lawrence Township's] highly successful model of a professional learning community through coaching by a cadre of expert practitioners situated in schools is important. Also of note is [Lawrence Township's] recognition of the systemic shifts required of leadership and school culture in order to institute reform of this depth and magnitude—and the time it takes for such shifts.

As Lemke recognizes, Lawrence Township is deeply immersed in and committed to the challenges of systemic change within a large organization. The words of Michael Fullan, a well-known scholar of education, best describe the district's perspective on leading the change process at this point: "Leading in a culture of change means creating a culture (not just a structure) of change. It does not mean adopting innovations, one after another; it does mean producing the capacity to seek, critically assess, and selectively incorporate new ideas and practices—all the time, inside the organization as well as outside it."[5] As Lawrence Township moves into the next phase of implementation, it is ultimately the "capacity to seek, critically assess, and selectively incorporate new ideas and practices" that will embed and institutionalize the skills of twenty-first century learning.

Notes

1. Wenglinsky, H. (2000, October). *How teaching matters: Bringing the classroom back into the discussions of teacher quality.* Princeton, NJ: Educational Testing Service; Ferguson, R. (1991). "Paying for public education: New evidence on how and why money matters." *Harvard Journal of Legislation* (1991); Greenwald, R., Hedges, L. V., & Laine, R. D. (1996). The effect of school resources on student achievement. *Review of Educational Research, 66*(3), 361–396.

2. Edwards, J. L., and Green, K. E. (1997). *The effects of cognitive coaching on teacher efficacy and empowerment.* Research Report No. 1997-1. Evergreen, CO: Author.; Joyce, B., & Showers, B. (1980). Improving in-service training: The messages of research. Educational Leadership, 37, 379–385.

3. DuFour, R. (1998). Why look elsewhere: Improving schools from within. *The School Administrator, 2*(55), 24–28; DuFour, R., & Eaker, R. (2001). Professional learning communities at work: Best practices for enhancing student achievement. Bloomington, IN: Solution Tree, pp. 24–29.

4. American Society for Training and Development 2001, Wheaton 2000.

5. Fullan, M. (2001). *Leading in a culture of change.* Hoboken, NJ: Wiley, p. 44.

MARCIA CAPUANO *is assistant superintendent for curriculum and instruction at the Metropolitan School District of Lawrence Township, Indianapolis, Indiana.*

TROY KNODERER *is Digital Age Literacy Initiative coordinator for the Metropolitan School District of Lawrence Township, Indianapolis, Indiana.*

*Exemplary efforts at twenty-first century learning
in Massachusetts hold promise for overcoming per-
sistent educational challenges, including high school
dropouts and static schools.*

10

Twenty-first century learning in states: The case of the Massachusetts educational system

David P. Driscoll

THE MISSION AND VISION statements of most educational institutions usually share the same lofty goal: to prepare students academically and socially for the opportunities they will face in their future adult lives. Their main thrust is to help prepare young people to become high-skilled, active, and productive citizens who will someday make positive contributions to society and the world.

Unfortunately, this goal is not being met, and this generation is facing a crisis going largely unnoticed. Today's graduates appear to be the least prepared for the world outside high school than any other generation in history. Who is responsible? Everyone, from the educators to the students to parents to society at large.

The world is changing rapidly, and the needs of top employers get more demanding and difficult. There was a time when higher education institutions in the United States prepared the right mix of graduates for the job market, but that is no longer the case. Today, colleges and universities are graduating large numbers of

NEW DIRECTIONS FOR YOUTH DEVELOPMENT, NO. 110, SUMMER 2006 © WILEY PERIODICALS, INC.
Published online in Wiley InterScience (www.interscience.wiley.com) • DOI: 10.1002/yd.172

127

social science majors, but top business leaders say they are struggling to find engineers.

Even more disturbing are the dissipating options for students who drop out of high school or do graduate but never go on to college. As noted in other chapters of this volume as well, today's economy offers few well-paying jobs for people without college degrees. But consider these shameful dropout statistics: in Massachusetts, just 76 percent of the students who enter high school as freshmen ever graduate, and just 29 percent of that freshman class typically goes on to complete a four-year degree after high school. Nationwide, according to the National Center for Public Policy and Higher Education, the numbers are even worse: 68 percent of freshmen graduate high school and just 18 percent graduate from college.[1]

Many of these young people are being pulled from the classroom by external issues that often have little to do with academics. More than ever before, students are coping with social issues, problems with bullying, difficult family situations, or financial problems severe enough for them to give up on school to find a full-time job. In addition, in Massachusetts, the number of suspensions and expulsions is rising, and teachers at all levels say they are forced to take time from instruction to discipline, counsel, or otherwise assist their students. As these and other issues grow more common in the lives of students, public schools need to adapt to meet their complex needs.

Despite the changing demands of the business world, the global economy, and society as a whole, the concept of public schooling has changed little since the days of Horace Mann. School is still in session for only ten months out of the year, students are still in class for only five to six hours a day, and students go home each night wondering how what they have learned relates to their lives.

Although we have made progress, it is not enough. Massachusetts is receiving nationwide attention for being a leader in education reform: we lead the nation on the National Assessment of Educational Progress (NAEP) and SAT year after year, and scores have risen just about every year on our own statewide assessment test. But leading the nation means much less now that the United States lags so far behind other countries. The overall effectiveness of our schools has to be questioned when so many students are ill prepared for the world around them.

It is time for our public education system to step into the twenty-first century and for educators to stop using practices, programs, and procedures that no longer meet the needs of students. Instead, a new focus must be placed on engaging students in their learning and helping them cope with the outside influences that may otherwise stall their education.

Excellent examples of this effort by educators can be found in many communities. One example is at the Gates Intermediate School in Scituate, Massachusetts, where seventh and eighth graders are conducting research through the Mars Student Imaging Project funded by the National Aeronautics and Space Administration. By evaluating images sent to earth from the *Mars Odyssey*, one of three spacecrafts orbiting Mars, students are learning about outer space and Mars imaging software, but also how scientific proposals are developed, how to work in teams, and the importance of competitive peer review.

Another example is in our vocational schools. Today vocational school students who complete a training program in a particular trade or professional skill area and who earn their competency determination by passing MCAS can receive the certificate of occupational proficiency. This new opportunity has prompted academic and technical teachers to work together to develop joint projects to reinvigorate the vocational-technical curricula. Successful programs have been implemented in several communities, including a school-to-work program at the Blue Hills Regional Technical School. There, students are participating in short-term cooperative education-employment with local businesses to gain exposure to working professionals in their chosen fields.

Simple programs have also garnered high praise, such as the Toolbox program at the Greater Lawrence Regional Technical School. There, tools of the academic trade are kept in student toolboxes to help them understand that academic knowledge is another asset at their disposal.

NEW DIRECTIONS FOR YOUTH DEVELOPMENT • DOI: 10.1002/yd

Groups like the Boston-based Citizen Schools have taken this idea to the next level and are working to expose students to twenty-first century skills through active apprenticeships with professionals such as lawyers, Web designers, journalists, and architects. Citizen Schools is currently working in seven Massachusetts communities and is scaling up nationwide.

Through both in-school and after-school programs, teachers have made significant strides toward meeting the complex needs of their students. But these efforts alone are not enough. Educators need to adjust their curricula to include the problem-solving and critical thinking skills needed to equip students to meet the needs of twenty-first century employers.

Massachusetts has taken this on most recently by offering expanded learning time grants to communities willing to increase their learning time by a minimum of 30 percent each year. In all, twenty-one districts applied for the planning grant, and sixteen were selected. These districts proposed changes that will include extending the school day and implementing before- and after-school programs. Pending legislative approval, these communities will put their new schedules in place at the start of the 2006–2007 school year. As schools struggle to make sure students are learning the basics during the normal school day, extended hours of learning are an opportunity to engage young people in applying their skills, practicing them, and becoming good leaders and collaborators—necessary capacities for success in the twenty-first century.

Business leaders have made it very clear that they are looking for different skills in employees. The workplace of the twenty-first century requires a high level of science, mathematics, and oral and writing skills and the ability to think creatively, solve new problems, and work in teams. Young people will be judged on their communication skills and their flexibility, as well as the ability to organize their thoughts and their work and to multitask and use all forms of technology.

In focusing on these areas, teachers must work diligently to ensure their students are engaged in their learning. Students respond to activities that are motivating, interesting, hands-on, and relevant to their lives, not to lengthy lectures about topics to which they cannot relate.

As educators, we should learn from and build on the success of programs that are truly engaging youth and incorporating twenty-first century skills standards. How we teach going forward must be guided by the needs of the outside world and each child, not the routines of the past. But our efforts cannot end in the classroom. School officials need to look seriously at extending the school day or school year (or both), and parents need to take more responsibility for supporting the academic success of their children.

Public education has hit a crossroads. We can continue offering the same programs and activities currently getting mediocre results, especially among students of color or from poor backgrounds. Or we can change the way we think about schools, adapt to serve the changing needs of students better, and leave them well prepared for the demands of today's fast-paced, high-technology working world.

Clearly there is no choice. Our children deserve a chance to graduate academically, socially, and emotionally prepared to compete and succeed in the twenty-first century world awaiting them.

Note

1. National Center for Public Policy and Higher Education. (2004). *The educational pipeline: Big investment, big returns.* http://www.highereducation. org/reports/pipeline/pipeline.pdf.

DAVID P. DRISCOLL *is commissioner of education for the Commonwealth of Massachusetts, overseeing a network of 386 public school districts with 1,872 public schools enrolling more than 975,000 students.*

The "Learn by Doing" philosophy of 4-H is an
example, now more than one hundred years old, of
how out-of-school learning programs have been used
effectively to develop advanced skills among youth.

11

Twenty-first century learning after school: The case of 4-H

Cathann Kress

I pledge:

> My head to clearer thinking,
>
> My heart to greater loyalty,
>
> My hands to larger service, and
>
> My health to better living for my club, my community, my country and my world.

THIS PLEDGE, WHICH HAS been repeated by millions of youth, identifies the guiding principles and the outcomes for 4-H created over a century ago. 4-H Youth Development is an educational movement founded to create opportunities for youth to understand their dependence on nature's resources and to value the fullest development of hand, head, and heart. It originated in the 1900s as "four-square education": educational development, fellowship development, physical development, and moral development.

For more than one hundred years, 4-H has been responding to the question, What does it take to assist young people to become

NEW DIRECTIONS FOR YOUTH DEVELOPMENT, NO. 110, SUMMER 2006 © WILEY PERIODICALS, INC.
Published online in Wiley InterScience (www.interscience.wiley.com) • DOI: 10.1002/yd.173

healthy, problem-solving, constructive adults? In the Carnegie Report, *Great Transitions: Preparing Adolescents for a New Century*, thirty years' worth of research was synthesized to answer this question.[1] *Great Transitions* supports the work that has been part of 4-H's legacy and drives our program into the twenty-first century. The report articulates that youth must find a valued place in a constructive group that lasts over time and that they must learn how to form close, durable relationships. Youth must earn a sense of worth through their own efforts and achieve a reliable basis for making informed choices, including ways to build a healthy lifestyle. In addition, youth must express constructive curiosity and exploratory behavior and find ways to be useful to others, they must believe in a future with real opportunities, and they must cultivate inquiring and problem-solving habits of the mind. Finally, youth need meaningful and engaging opportunities to learn to respect democratic values and citizenship.

A century ago, while economic prosperity generally characterized American agriculture, there was a lack of opportunity for rural children that would propel them to a better quality of life. In this atmosphere of prosperity tempered by concern for the future of a generation of rural children, the movement that became 4-H evolved. From its inception, this American idea—the 4-H Youth Development movement—was about creating opportunities for youth to learn about the natural world, technology, themselves, and communities. 4-H, with its emphasis on learning by doing, began to impress on youth the importance of becoming lifelong learners.

Learning by doing

As the United States grew, public education was the cornerstone of this bold experiment in nation building, and 4-H connected youth to universities and the latest research being conducted. It became part of the larger effort on the part of the U.S. Department of Agriculture (USDA) to connect citizens to rapidly developing advances in agricultural sciences and technology discovered by the land grant universities. A major concept of this idea was learning by doing—to teach knowledge and life skills that enhance quality of life by exploring firsthand the practical matters of community and home life.

Leading by example

The pioneers who shaped 4-H began with the belief that changing youth would change the nation. In 4-H, as the land grant university knowledge was extended to youth, they responded by becoming early adopters of technology and research. In fact, America has become strong due in part to the rapid rate of technology transfer from laboratories to practice. Throughout its history, 4-H has been a leader in creating the access and opportunity that lead youth to consistently serve as those early adopters.

4-H today

The 4-H idea is alive and well in all fifty states, the territories, and army installations worldwide, where 4-H takes university knowledge and expertise to youth in rural, suburban, and urban communities. Today, 45 percent of youth reached by 4-H are from rural areas and small towns, and 55 percent are from the suburbs and large inner cities. These youth are often among the first to learn about new scientific discoveries and related technologies and to apply them in real-world settings with their projects.

Hands-on projects range from citizenship to expressive arts, consumer science, environmental education, leadership, and technology, as well as animal and plant sciences. Over 7 million youth, ages five to twenty, participate in 4-H experiences. According to a study in New York, youth in 4-H do better in school than other students, are more motivated to help others, and are developing skills in leadership, public speaking, self-esteem, communication, and planning, and are making lasting friendships.[2] These findings have been supported in studies from Montana[3] and Colorado[4] as well.

What America needs from 4-H in the twenty-first century

The core of 4-H—meeting youth needs and building life skills—is timeless and unchanging. It is as relevant today early in the twenty-first century as it was at the previous turn of the century when 4-H was developed to teach farming practices and food preservation techniques. But how we meet youth needs and build life skills continually changes. And what we teach—the new technology, the latest advancements from universities—also changes. We believe the United States needs 4-H to continue creating opportunities for youth much as it has always done. For example, due to the approaching retirements of scientists in the baby boom generation, the Department of Labor predicts that within ten years, the workplace will be 6 million people short of the 18 million needed to replace those scientists. Another great need is to continue informing the public about science that is important to our daily lives.

In 2001, only about 50 percent of adults surveyed by the National Science Foundation knew that it takes the earth one year to go around the sun, that humans did not live at the same time as dinosaurs, or that antibiotics do not kill viruses.[5] In 4-H, youth are actively engaged in science, from assessing water quality to determining DNA, from interpreting ultrasound images to predicting the impact of zero gravity environments on everyday objects. The opportunities to learn how to think, plan, and reason are endless.

The foundation of 4-H is in the practical application of the knowledge base generated from the land grant university system and USDA by youth in their communities. Perhaps more than ever before, in today's world with its increasing complexity, America also needs youth prepared to become leaders and active community citizens who are understanding, compassionate, and value life. The 4-H pledge focuses on these ideals.

"I pledge my head to clearer thinking"

Youth need to know that they are able to influence people and events through decision making and action. In fact, independence is the flip side of the coin of responsibility. If we want responsible youth, we must give them increasing independence. By exercising independence through 4-H leadership opportunities, youth mature in self-discipline and responsibility and learn to better understand themselves and become independent thinkers. In Oregon, the Attitudes for Success Youth Leadership Program was developed to provide opportunities for Hispanic youth to develop life skills and community involvement. A coalition of county agencies, parents, and youth met to discuss the needs of area Hispanic families and develop strategies to provide positive experiences for these individuals. With a 30 percent Hispanic high school dropout rate in the Umatilla/Morrow Education Service District, it was determined that there was a need for Hispanics to learn about community leadership and college opportunities. The program consists of two parts: an annual day-long leadership and college preparation conference and a youth leadership board experience that provides intensive leadership opportunities on a monthly basis.

Youth need to learn that decisions made should be considered carefully and acted on only after the implications of those decisions are explored and weighed. Youth are given leadership positions in 4-H clubs that allow them to work with other members and take responsibility for many of the decisions and actions that were once solely those of adults. Organizational skills, patience, and group dynamics are key traits learned that become assets to youth as they mature into contributing adults. Youth are not just the leaders of tomorrow; they have great untapped potential for responsible leadership today.

"I pledge my heart to greater loyalty"

Youth need to know they are cared about by others and feel a sense of connection. This fellowship has always been an important part of a 4-H experience. Current research emphasizes the importance for youth to have opportunities for long-term, consistent relationships with adults other than parents. This research suggests that a sense of belonging may be the most powerful positive ingredient we can add to the lives of youth. Success in life rarely comes to an individual without some type of personal interaction with others. Working in groups through 4-H strengthens and reinforces social skills that will allow youth to coexist and thrive with others in society.

In Missouri, the 4-H program fosters these connections by helping families of incarcerated men and women, particularly those with children, who struggle with insufficient family programs and parent-child separation. The 4-H LIFE program offers the opportunity to break the cycle of incarceration and remove barriers between offenders and their families by creating opportunities for children and youth to overcome some of the challenges of parental incarceration. The program was developed jointly by the incarcerated parents and local 4-H staff to address the needs of the children. Project LIFE consists of 4-H educational activities and parenting training. At monthly meetings, children, parents, and caregivers work together on traditional 4-H club activities and hands-on projects in order to develop life skills.

"I pledge my health to better living"

To develop self-confidence, youth need to believe they are capable and must experience success at solving problems and meeting challenges. They need a safe environment for making mistakes and getting feedback, not just through competition but also as an ongoing element of participation. Through 4-H, members are given the opportunity to explore interests or possibilities for future careers.

One example is Seeds to Success, an entrepreneurial and life skills training program in New Jersey, preparing at-risk fourteen to eighteen year olds for the workforce. Through classroom education during the school year and on-the-job training, these teens are better able to take charge of their futures and become active, contributing members of the workforce and their communities. The program objectives are to teach special-needs youth how to select and prepare locally grown fruits and vegetables for use in meal preparation and how to handle money and banking procedures, and to provide them opportunities to acquire workforce readiness and business skills by selling produce at a youth-run farmstand during summer months.

It is just as important for youth to discover in a nonthreatening setting that certain vocations may not be right for them. Many 4-H alumni report that the enjoyment and sense of mastery they experienced through successful 4-H project work laid the seed for future employment.

"I pledge my hands to larger service"

Youth need to feel their lives have meaning and purpose. By participating in 4-H citizenship activities, youth connect to communities and learn to give back to others. These experiences provide the foundation that help youth understand the big picture of life. They learn that they do not live in a secluded world; instead, they are part of a global community, which requires awareness and compassion for others. 4-H members involved in Teen 24/7 Tech Club at Fort Campbell, Kentucky, experienced this service-learning using the latest in technology. Youth, adult leaders, and volunteers worked together to provide information for 911 and Homeland Security. Working with the Hopkinsville Planning Commission, they used global positioning system units and global imaging system software to plot and map mile markers on the railroad that runs through Fort Campbell and Hopkinsville. Because this railroad is used to ship military equipment and supplies, the commission needed the information available in satellite mapping form. The youth participating in this project learned not only how to use this technology; they also assisted a local agency in providing useful information for national purposes. The next project for this 4-H group will be using the same technology to map street signs along a busy section of Hopkinsville's Fort Campbell Boulevard. The information gathered will be used to assist the planning commission in deciding where and when signs need to be replaced or repositioned.

4-H programs focus youth on developing concern for others and taking meaningful action to demonstrate that concern. Whether through the Victory Gardens of the 1940s or the outpouring of service after 9/11, the partnerships between clubs after Hurricane

Katrina or the everyday efforts important to the fabric of local communities, these projects keep roadsides clean, restore old cemeteries, and gather food for the less fortunate. Meaningful service forges bonds between youth and the community, and doing something that others value raises feelings of self-worth and competence.

Conclusion

If no youth development programs existed and we were to develop one intended to assist young people to become healthy, problem-solving, constructive adults and based our efforts on the latest research, it would offer opportunities for belonging. It would offer opportunities to experience that hands-on laboratory for a mastery of ideas that are relevant in today's world. It would offer opportunities for young people to choose. It would offer meaningful opportunities to experience what it means to be an engaged citizen. It would look a lot like 4-H.

Notes

1. Carnegie Council for Adolescent Development (1995). *Great transitions: Preparing adolescents for a new century.* New York: Carnegie Corporation.

2. Rodriguez, E., Hirschl, T., Mead, J., & Goggin, S. (1999). *Understanding the difference 4-H clubs make in the lives of New York youth: How 4-H contributes to positive youth development.* Ithaca, NY: Cornell University. http://nys4h-staff.cce.cornell.edu/4-HClubStudy.htm.

3. Astroth, K., & Haynes, G. (2002). More than cows and cooking: New research shows the impact of 4-H. *Journal of Extension, 40*(4). http://www.joe.org/joe/2002august/a6.shtml.

4. Goodwin, J., Carroll, J., & Oliver, M. (2005). *Measuring the impact of Colorado's 4-H Youth Development Program.* Fort Collins: Colorado State University.

5. National Science Board. (2002). *Science and engineering indicators, 2002.* (NSB-02-1) Arlington, VA: National Science Foundation.

CATHANN KRESS *is director of youth development for National 4-H Headquarters, Cooperative State Research, Education, and Extension Service at the U.S. Department of Agriculture. 4-H is the largest out-of-school youth program in the United States, with more than 7 million members and 500,000 teen and adult volunteers.*

Junior Achievement has begun to incorporate twenty-first century skills into its business and entrepreneurship curriculum for youth in its K–12 school and after-school programs.

12

Twenty-first century learning after school: The case of Junior Achievement Worldwide

John M. Box

INCREASED ATTENTION TO developing after-school programs for America's youth is indicative of a national desire to provide safe environments in which to extend the learning that takes place during a typical school day. The growing need for and benefit of such programs is demonstrable. A study conducted by the Afterschool Alliance reveals that 14.3 million children take care of themselves after the school day ends, including almost 4 million middle school students in grades 6 through 8. Just 6.5 million children are in after-school programs; however, parents of another 15.3 million children say their children would participate in an after-school program if one were available.[1]

It is not enough, however, simply to provide young people with safe after-school environments. The content of programs offered in these settings must contribute to each young person's future success. According to the U.S. Departments of Education and

NEW DIRECTIONS FOR YOUTH DEVELOPMENT, NO. 110, SUMMER 2006 © WILEY PERIODICALS, INC.
Published online in Wiley InterScience (www.interscience.wiley.com) • DOI: 10.1002/yd.174

Justice, students in quality after-school programs have better academic performance, behavior, and school attendance and greater expectations for the future than those who do not participate in such programs.[2]

JA Worldwide (JA) serves as a leader in the development and implementation of quality after-school programs for young people around the globe. JA is the world's largest organization dedicated to educating young people about business, economics, and free enterprise. Volunteers teach JA programs in classrooms and after-school locations throughout the United States and in one hundred other countries. JA has provided quality after-school opportunities for eighty-six years, beginning with its first program introduced to America's youth in 1919. While JA now offers students in kindergarten through high school twenty-four different classroom-based, after-school, and capstone programs, the organization remains deeply rooted in the after-school arena.

JA understands that for any educational program to be truly effective, it must provide young people with learning that prepares them for success in the twenty-first century. The definition of twenty-first century learning as proposed by the Partnership for 21st Century Skills resonates strongly with JA and has provided a template for developing programs that will lead to this future success.

It is important to summarize the six components of twenty-first century learning identified by the partnership:[3]

1. *Emphasis on core subjects.* Twenty-first century learning takes place when students receive instruction in English, reading or language arts, mathematics, science, foreign languages, civics, government, economics, history, geography, and the arts that goes beyond basic competency. It requires young people to understand core academic content at much higher levels.

2. *Teaching and learning twenty-first century content.* Content that is critical to success in communities and workplaces typically is not emphasized in schools today. Twenty-first century content includes

global awareness; financial, economic, business, and entrepreneurial understanding; and civic literacy.

3. *Teaching and learning in a twenty-first century context.* Twenty-
first century learning requires that students learn academic content
through real-world examples, applications, and experiences both
inside and outside schools.

4. *Emphasis on learning skills.* Twenty-first century learning
relies on developing the skills that promote life-long learning.
These include information and communication skills, thinking and
problem-solving skills, creativity and innovation skills, and interpersonal and self-directional skills.

5. *Use of twenty-first century tools to develop learning skills.* Twenty-
first century learning relies on providing the information and communication technology tools essential to everyday life and
workplace productivity.

6. *Using twenty-first century assessments to measure twenty-first century skills.* More authentic assessment measures are essential in measuring twenty-first century learning. Assessment must measure each
component that defines this learning.

As existing programs are revised and new ones developed, JA
concentrates on building content around the knowledge, skills, and
attitudes students need to succeed in this century. Program design
is based on identifying what students should know and be able to
accomplish as they learn about free enterprise. As a frame of reference for its program development, JA has embraced the key tenets
of twenty-first century learning proposed by the partnership.
Specifically, JA programs teach twenty-first century content in a
twenty-first century context, emphasize twenty-first century learning skills, and use twenty-first century learning tools.

JA's success in providing after-school programs is the result of
purpose guiding development and implementation. JA Worldwide's
mission—to ensure that every child has a fundamental understanding of the free enterprise system—is realized by designing
programs around twenty-first century content in seven key areas:

business, citizenship, economics, entrepreneurship, ethics and character, financial literacy, and career development.

The first JA after-school program, now titled JA Company Program, has inspired more than four million high school students to appreciate and better understand the role of business in society. Through JA Company Program, students organize and operate an actual business enterprise. This experience helps them not only learn how businesses function but also teaches them about the structure of the U.S. free enterprise system and the benefits it provides.

It is easy to see how twenty-first century learning is supported through involvement in this program. Following is a representative list of the twenty-first century learning that students participating in the program receive. Students:

- Analyze and explore personal opportunities and responsibilities within a company.
- Design company strategies that include business production, financial, and marketing plans.
- Produce a product, monitor productivity, evaluate product quality, and create a selling strategy.
- Develop an annual report for stockholders, and go through the process of liquidating their company.

In July 2005, JA Worldwide launched its first after-school program for elementary school children. JA Dollars and $ense teaches students in grades 3 through 5 about earning, spending, sharing, and saving money. Through their involvement in this program, students learn about businesses they can start and jobs they can perform to earn money. JA It's My Business! the organization's first after-school program designed for middle grade students, was introduced in June 2006. By providing engaging, academically enriching, experiential learning focused on entrepreneurship, the program meets the needs of a diverse group of students. JA Dollars and $ense and JA It's My Business! also promote twenty-first century learning through the activities that are included in each of these programs.

Through JA Dollars and $ense, students in grades 3 to 5:

- Learn to manage a personal bank account by identifying the role of money in everyday life, understanding the benefits of a bank account, practice making sound financial decisions, and manage deposits and withdrawals.
- Identify the characteristics of a positive work ethic, distinguish between working for someone else and self-employment, identify ways to earn income through jobs or a small business, and practice personal money management skills and ethical decision making.
- Identify personal skills and interests and connect them with possible business opportunities, identify the basic steps for starting and operating a small business, and develop a business plan.
- Learn concepts related to consumer decision making by learning to recognize deceptive advertising and the importance of ethical business practices.

Through JA It's My Business! middle grade students:

- Develop an understanding of the entrepreneurial characteristics they possess by learning about the lives of past and present entrepreneurs.
- Identify the knowledge and skills needed to create a product or business and use this information to consider customer needs as a prerequisite to developing a product design.
- Analyze current examples of social entrepreneurs to identify businesses they can start and examine ways entrepreneurs focus their skill and passion on creating products to improve the lives of others.
- Create commercials for unique products and businesses and identify ways to market those products and businesses to a variety of audiences.
- Apply their knowledge of entrepreneurs and entrepreneurial characteristics by creating their own personal vision for the future.

JA also recognizes that after-school programs cannot present to students more of what they already receive during regular classroom hours. To be effective, after-school initiatives must engage students actively in the learning that takes place. Thus, each JA program is taught in a twenty-first century context by providing students with real-life, hands-on learning experiences taught by a trained volunteer from the business community. Volunteer involvement provides an additional benefit for students in that volunteers also serve as role models for the young people they teach and, through their personal experiences, are able to bring the program content to life. The success of this method of program delivery has established strong school-business partnerships across the United States. Again, that these partnerships work so well in teaching twenty-first century skills is the main point because of the unique advantage of leveraging the intellectual capital and experience of the modern workforce toward education.

Further contributing to its success is JA's commitment to evaluating the effectiveness of its programs. Over the past ten years, external program evaluations confirm that JA programs increase student knowledge of business and economic principles, increase student understanding of the free enterprise system, and contribute to students' positive attitudes, behaviors, and aspirations. The outcomes of these evaluations substantially reinforce the importance of building programs around twenty-first century learning.

Education in the United States will not shape a new generation of workforce and civic leaders until the knowledge, skills, and attitudes students require for success become the norm rather than the exception. Making twenty-first century learning the standard will be realized when educational programs offer students hands-on, real-life experiences that mirror what they will encounter when they leave school and enter a career. Moving forward with its after-school initiatives, JA Worldwide continues to provide the twenty-first century learning all students will need to prosper in tomorrow's world.

NEW DIRECTIONS FOR YOUTH DEVELOPMENT • DOI: 10.1002/yd

Notes

1. U.S. Department of Education. (2000). *After-school programs: Keeping children safe and smart*. Washington, DC: U.S. Department of Education. http://www.ed.gov/pubs/afterschool/afterschool.pdf.

2. Afterschool Alliance. (2003). *America after 3 PM*. Washington, DC: Afterschool Alliance. http://www.afterschoolalliance.org/america_3pm.cfm.

3. Partnership for 21st Century Skills. (2003). *Learning for the twenty-first century: A report and MILE guide for twenty-first century skills*. Washington, DC: Partnership for 21st Century Skills. http://www.twenty-firstcentury skills.org.

JOHN M. BOX *is vice president of product development for Junior Achievement Worldwide, the world's largest organization dedicated to educating young people about business, economics, and entrepreneurship through in-school and after-school programs for students in grades K–12.*

For twenty-first century learning to take hold in schools, teachers must be empowered with the training and infrastructure necessary to incorporate new skills into the classroom.

13

Twenty-first century learning for teachers: Helping educators bring new skills into the classroom

John I. Wilson

THE NATIONAL EDUCATION ASSOCIATION's active involvement in the Partnership for 21st Century Skills flows naturally from the focus of all our work: supporting educational employees so they can enable students to succeed in life. At times, with all the focus on accountability, test scores, and school restructuring, we may lose sight of the ultimate goal of education: empowering all students to attain personal and professional success when they leave school. I intentionally say "leave school" rather than "complete their education," because clearly lifelong learning is a threshold competency in this century.

When we present the partnership's framework to our members, the response is always enthusiastic and positive, though at times tempered by frustration that too few schools are adequately equipped to meet these goals. Members tell us they want both the physical and policy infrastructures that promote this kind of learning. They want the professional development and curricular materials that facilitate

NEW DIRECTIONS FOR YOUTH DEVELOPMENT, NO. 110, SUMMER 2006 © WILEY PERIODICALS, INC.
Published online in Wiley InterScience (www.interscience.wiley.com) • DOI: 10.1002/yd.175

it. And, critically, they want assessments that can meaningfully measure the outcomes outlined in the partnership's work.

Twenty-first century skills

Ubiquitous information technology and the need to be technologically literate are major components of this new approach to learning. However, the greatest challenges may come not from the technology itself but from the ensuing functionalities it enables. Students must be able to sagely navigate and contribute to the massive electronic information flow that is central to society today. They must make key decisions in a rapid-paced 24/7 environment and bring global context to their understanding of the world around them. They consistently must be able to retool to accommodate constant change and ever evolving technology. These kinds of skills are not isolated from our normal functions outside school, and they should not be isolated within school. Our overall instruction across subject areas, as well as our standards and assessments, must reflect the tools, functionalities, content, and context of the world in which we live.

These new challenges pose significant new responsibilities for schools and educators. They also offer educational employees the kind of exhilarating opportunities that attracted them to the field. Educators want to equip students, not simply fill them with data. Educators want their classrooms to be the entry point, not the confines, of their students' understanding of the world. Educators recognize that whether a student lives in a remote location in the prairies, an inner-city neighborhood, or a cosmopolitan suburb, he or she will need highly developed skills to fully participate in today's global economy and society.

First steps

We do this in the same way we nurture anything: by creating a supportive and enabling environment. First, we must ask these questions:

- Do our educational standards across subject areas incorporate the realities of today's world?
- Do we measure what is easiest to assess or what will really determine a student's ability to succeed in the future?
- Do we provide students and educators the tools and environments that match those outside school building walls?
- Do educational employees—administrators, school support personnel, teachers—have adequate time and access to consistent professional development so they can retool to meet the evolving challenges of the world?
- Do civic leaders, corporate leaders, and educators regularly partner to ensure that schools reflect the needs and demands of the world around them and are equipped to meet them?
- Do we use new technologies and approaches to ensure that achievement gaps—based on economics, ethnicity, race, gender, or physical capacity—are eliminated, and not exacerbated, in this new era?
- Do we sufficiently acknowledge that when we are discussing investments in education, what we are really talking about is the future of our nation?

Educational strategies

Next, we should look for specific strategies and examples that can guide us through this transformation. As the partnership materials affirm, core competencies, if anything, are even more critical now, but they must be taught with contemporary tools and context. To illustrate and guide schools, the partnership has issued literacy maps that demonstrate how traditional subject areas, such as mathematics and English, can be taught so they are relevant to students and equip them with the lifelong skills they will need:

  • The math map, created in collaboration with the National Council of Teachers of Mathematics, outlines how mathematics education at various grade levels can incorporate both modern technological tools as well as such skills as team building, critical thinking, and problem solving.

• The English map, created with the National Council of Teachers of English, shows how media literacy, Internet research, and multimedia creations are all part of a robust English educational program.

• The geography guide, produced with the National Council for Geographic Education, describes such activities for students as using "a geographic information system to identify the best location for a new park according to defined criteria" or creating "innovative plans, including specific recommendations illustrated by maps, to improve the quality of environments in large cities, weighing the benefits and drawbacks of each plan." Students learn geography and in the process also learn how to think, collaborate, interpret information, and communicate effectively.

• The science map, coproduced with the National Association of Science Teachers, reveals how students can use simulation software or Internet collaboration tools for problem solving in that field. In learning science content, they are developing technology literacy, as well as problem solving and communications skills.

These all demonstrate that infusing these skills into content areas enriches the content and better engages students by using interactive instruments and materials relevant to the world outside the school building. We do not have to choose between traditional content areas and twenty-first century skills, but can enhance the delivery of both through incorporating these skills into content instruction.

We must also more fully explore twenty-first century approaches to assessment. First, we must ensure that assessment tools are based on our values, not our convenience. Second, we must more fully explore the potential for assessment beyond its role as an accountability instrument. Technology should be exploited so that assessment can be a powerful tool in a classroom teacher's daily instructional practice. And while technology is not the focus of twenty-first century education, comprehensive access to the tools of this century is part of the infrastructure necessary for this learning to occur.

Public policy

Educators welcome this framework for learning. They know that all students must have highly developed problem-solving, analytical, and communications skills and must understand the global community in which they live. Educators do not need to be convinced of the value of this approach to learning, but they do need policy underpinnings that support it.

Educational standards must incorporate these critical skills, and then curriculum and assessments must align with these twenty-first century standards. Professional development programs must help teachers meet these new educational goals, and educational employees must have time and access to quality programs that support their efforts to provide twenty-first century education. The physical infrastructure and tools of our schools must mirror those of the world outside school.

The actual cost of these measures is dwarfed by the staggering price to our economic and civic well-being of not implementing them. Around the world, other nations are reengineering their educational systems to meet the emerging demands of contemporary life. If we fail to act, we will lose ground in the global society.

Conclusion

Everyone who works in a school relishes the daily successes they see among students and agonizes over the apparent failures. Student achievement in quantifiable and less easily quantifiable ways is the lifeblood of educators' lives. It keeps them motivated, even under difficult circumstances. However, what most elates an educator, and makes the hard work, long hours, and occasional frustrations worthwhile, is to learn that a former student has not simply succeeded on a test but has succeeded in life. That is our mission. That is why we wake up every morning and enter frequently challenging environments to accomplish our work. And that is why ensuring students are prepared for the demands of today's world is at the core of the work of the National Education Association. What is the purpose of American education if not to prepare students to meet the real challenges of this century?

JOHN I. WILSON *is executive director of the National Education Association, the nation's largest professional employee organization, representing 2.7 million elementary and secondary teachers, college faculty, school administrators, education support professionals, retired educators, and students preparing to become teachers.*

NEW DIRECTIONS FOR YOUTH DEVELOPMENT • DOI: 10.1002/yd

A range of real-world projects after school in data analysis, writing, problem solving, and oral communication helps an immigrant girl fulfill her father's promise of a good education for a better life.

14

Twenty-first century skills for students: Hands-on learning after school builds school and life success

Leide Cabral

I AM A STUDENT WHO, through my formal education, life experiences, extracurricular activities, and enrichment and after-school programs, has developed and used twenty-first century skills. I have had to work hard to get to where I am. I am a student headed to a good college on a full scholarship, and I am a future leader in society. I am a student of the twenty-first century. I am not afraid of technology, and I love learning and adapting to new things. It has been through opportunities where I have developed skills such as leadership, oral and written communication, and data analysis, as well as opportunities where I have been recognized for these skills, that I have expanded my educational horizons and my life ambitions.

When I was four, I came to America from a little island off the coast of Africa called Cape Verde. I came with my father. We settled in a strong Cape Verdean community in Boston where several

NEW DIRECTIONS FOR YOUTH DEVELOPMENT, NO. 110, SUMMER 2006 © WILEY PERIODICALS, INC.
Published online in Wiley InterScience (www.interscience.wiley.com) • DOI: 10.1002/yd.176

of my aunts and uncles already lived. My father and I joined them and began the process of establishing our lives in America. Although living in an area with a great number of Cape Verdeans made fitting in easier, it did not make finding a job easier, and my father struggled with this for a while. He had only a high school education, which made things difficult. But eventually my father was able to find a job in a nearby town, at a manufacturing company.

Although I grew up with my extended family, it was just my father and me until at age ten my stepmother came into our lives. Although she has been an influence in my life, it is really my father who has supported me as I have grown up in Boston. My stepmother is now struggling to get her GED while raising my two sisters and my brother.

By the time I entered school I had already learned a lot from the experience of immigrating to the United States. Big changes, even at such a young age, impact you and make you grow. Our family feels that getting a good education is essential for success. My father has been working hard his whole life so that I might have the chance to attend college and have better opportunities than he had. Knowing this drives me to do my best.

From the time I settled here until the present day I have been in the Boston Public Schools system. The Boston Public Schools system is very diverse and full of teachers who have inspired me. Boston is one big mix of cultural backgrounds: 24 percent of the population is African American, 14 percent is Hispanic or Latino, 8 percent is Asian, and only 49 percent of the population is Caucasian. In Boston today we strive to respect each other and acknowledge our differences. In my high school, Boston Latin School, we try to learn about each other's cultures and celebrate them. There are dozens of clubs where students organize around their cultural background, and we integrate them as often as possible, whether in performances, festivals, or just mixed meetings. These cultural clubs, however, are not strictly for students from specific backgrounds: the best thing about them is that anyone can join. I am president of the Cape Verdean Club. I value helping to bring together and lead a cross-cultural community of students.

NEW DIRECTIONS FOR YOUTH DEVELOPMENT • DOI: 10.1002/yd

With my family history, my life experiences, my schooling, the roles I have played in my education, and the wide variety of sources from which my learning has come, it is safe to say that skills in life come from everywhere. Education has changed so much and now influences the way people learn and the skills they need, in addition to the traditional curriculum of school, in order to succeed. I am an example of someone who has grown so much through learning, developing, and using twenty-first century skills. My cultural and family background I have just described, and the other aspects of my education that make school an experience both in and outside of the classroom, are just the beginning of how I have worked to develop the skills it will take for me to excel in the twenty-first century.

Data analysis and writing

In the sixth grade I joined Citizen Schools, an after-school education program that focuses on hands-on learning apprenticeships and homework help. In Citizen Schools, students get experiences in both large and small groups, working together on projects. We each have a team of students who work together and with a Citizen Schools staff member who serves as a team leader. In eighth grade I entered Citizen Schools' Eighth Grade Academy, a special program that helped me with data analysis and writing skills to prepare me for high school. It is in Citizen Schools that I really began building my twenty-first century skills.

Many families in Boston are unable to navigate the Boston Public Schools system and offer their children the education they could have. They often lack the information and access it takes to have a strong role in their family's schooling—and even more often, they lack the time to try to access this information, let alone understand it. In Boston, students are given the opportunity to choose which high school they want to attend. Many families end up believing that all high schools are the same; this is false. There are high schools that have very high academic standards and high schools that focus more on vocational skills. Depending on what a student plans to do when he or she grows up, a high school that focuses on his or her goals makes a huge difference. Making the right kinds of choices in cases like this one is crucial.

At Citizen Schools I was able to analyze Boston Public Schools statistics in order to select the best high school to attend. I looked at drop-out rates as well as at passing rates for MCAS, an exam every student in Massachusetts must take and pass in order to graduate from high school. I also compared how many of the graduating students attend a four-year college. After I collected the data, I discussed it with my group and team leader, eventually making bar graphs and pie charts so that I could visually compare the information. In the end we concluded which schools would most help us get on a college track and develop high academic standards and a mind-set for life-long learning and success. This was an experience and exercise that developed not only my data analysis skills but my collective learning skills as well. What is more, I was able to practice my learning and teach it back, as I was then able to inform my family of the data I had gathered, giving them access to information about working with what the Boston school system has to offer. I was taking a hold on my education and helping to guide my family.

Citizen Schools' Eighth Grade Academy puts a very strong emphasis on writing skills. As a part of their Writing Program, I was paired up with a lawyer from Goodwin Procter law firm, Michael Tabachnick, who became my writing coach. When Michael told me to write an essay about any topic, I chose to write about why there should not be a limit on the amount of homework a teacher assigns. I picked this topic because the school I was attending hardly gave homework. I strongly feel that the best way to learn is to practice; homework is practicing what the teacher taught you that day. Michael not only helped me express this topic of concern, he also helped me improve my overall writing skills. By the end of each session with him I felt more and more confident in my essay-writing ability, a crucial skill for success in high school. My final product, my opinion in a five-hundred-word, high school-level, persuasive essay, was published in the Citizen Schools' Eighth

Grade Academy magazine, *Bridging*. Thinking back on what I gained from this experience, I know that while I learned a great deal from my writing coach, I also taught him as well—through our educational partnership we learned from each other.

The twenty-first century data analysis, writing, teamwork, and leadership skills I obtained from these experiences have helped me in high school and life. Boston Latin School is known for being the first public school in America. To its students in Boston, it is known for its high academic standards and huge workload. Coming from Citizen Schools' Eighth Grade Academy and carrying with me what I learned, I felt prepared to enter the Latin school. Although I struggled with the great amount of work, my writing skills really helped me write the "one-a-day" essays every student must complete, and my data analysis skills helped me start off my algebra experience with an A on my first test!

Oral communication and leadership

My experiences with Citizen Schools in middle school gave me confidence. At my middle school, I was seen as the shy girl who did her work but hardly raised her hand in class. This changed after I participated in a mock trial "apprenticeship," our after-school course with Citizen Schools led by a volunteer. During this apprenticeship, students are paired with lawyers to learn how to plan for and perform at an imitation trial. By the end, the students conduct a trial in a real courtroom with a judge and witnesses. As one of the lawyers in the trial, I had to make an opening speech to persuade the jury, question a witness in a one-on-one interview, and defend my client in a courtroom full of my peers, adults, and lawyers. When I was preparing my speech for the mock trial I had to focus on the audience and decide what approach to the topic would best grab their attention. I also had to figure out what my tone should be and if hand movements would add to my speech or distract the audience. When I finally delivered my speech, I was surprised—but mostly pleased and proud—at the booming, attention-grabbing voice that came from *me*.

NEW DIRECTIONS FOR YOUTH DEVELOPMENT • DOI: 10.1002/yd

The twenty-first century skills I learned and practiced to make that speech in middle school—oral communication and logical thinking—are skills I still use today. In August 2005 I gave a speech to a group of four hundred new Boston Public Schools teachers about my life and how the Boston Public Schools system has affected it, making myself a resource to them as they started their careers. I was able to articulately discuss myself and my views on educational issues with confidence. Public speaking skills have also helped me in the classroom. This year my English teacher gave an assignment in which we had to research a topic, write an essay, and then give a persuasive speech, with only a small note card for assistance. I earned an A on the assignment.

Another twenty-first century skill I have been developing is leadership. As president of the Cape Verdean Club at Boston Latin School, I have many responsibilities. I am responsible for planning the meetings, informing the members, managing money for costumes, arranging shows, and much more. Organizational skills, social skills, management skills, and especially creativity really help me accomplish these tasks.

My present and my future

Now that I have graduated from Citizen Schools, I volunteer. In an effort to be socially responsible, I give back as a deputy team leader for the program. It is my responsibility to attend the program every Saturday morning at 8:00 A.M. in order to assist the team leaders in running workshops and activities. I am expected to be a role model for the students. On occasion I am given the opportunity to actually teach a lesson. Before each lesson I make sure to look at the schedule and review the material so I know it well enough to teach and answer questions. I have realized through teaching that the secret to obtaining leadership skills is being able to take initiative. When I notice that students do not completely comprehend a problem, I take initiative and try to explain differently. As a deputy team leader, it is my responsibility to see what needs to be done and to do it efficiently.

Before I was able to develop and expand my confidence, thinking, and ability at Citizen Schools, I was an underachieving student with unrealized potential—a common problem plaguing students, schools, and families across America. After graduating from Citizen Schools' Eighth Grade Academy, I attended Boston Latin School. I am now a senior. I will be attending Hamilton College this fall with a Posse Scholarship—a full-tuition, four-year paid leadership scholarship.

Six years ago the thought of college was vague and unrealistic. My father would often tell me stories of how he was accepted into a college in Portugal but was not able to attend because he wanted me to have a better life in America. He gave up his dream of higher education to make sure that I would have better opportunities. I now know that the sacrifices he made were worth it. The networks I have developed over the last six years—at Citizen Schools, at Boston Latin School, in my Cape Verdean Club, on my soccer and track teams, at the Posse Foundation, in my community, and countless other places—will help support me. The life-learning and twenty-first century skills I have acquired and embraced—team building, leadership, writing and oral communication, data analysis, practicing and teaching, and creative thinking—will help me succeed.

LEIDE CABRAL *recently graduated from Boston Latin School, one of Boston's premier exam high schools, and is an alumna of Citizen Schools' after-school education program. She is currently attending Hamilton College in New York on full scholarship.*

Index

Notes for Contributors

After reading this issue, you might be inspired to become a contributor. *New Directions for Youth Development: Theory, Practice, and Research* is a quarterly publication focusing on contemporary issues inspiring and challenging the field of youth development. A defining focus of the journal is the relationship among theory, research, and practice. In particular, *NDYD* is dedicated to recognizing resilience as well as risk, and healthy development of our youth as well as the difficulties of adolescence. The journal is intended as a forum for provocative discussion that reaches across the worlds of academia, service, philanthropy, and policy.

In the tradition of the New Directions series, each volume of the journal addresses a single, timely topic, although special issues covering a variety of topics are occasionally commissioned. We welcome submissions of both volume topics and individual articles. All articles should address the implications of theory for practice and research directions, and how these arenas can better inform one another. Articles may focus on any aspect of youth development; all theoretical and methodological orientations are welcome.

If you would like to be an *issue editor,* please submit an outline of no more than four pages that includes a brief description of your proposed topic and its significance along with a brief synopsis of individual articles (including tentative authors and a working title for each chapter).

If you would like to be an *author,* please submit first a draft of an abstract of no more than 1,500 words, including a two-sentence synopsis of the article; send this to the editorial assistant.

For all prospective issue editors or authors:

- Please make sure to keep accessibility in mind, by illustrating theoretical ideas with specific examples and explaining technical terms in nontechnical language. A busy practitioner who may not have an extensive research background should be well served by our work.

- Please keep in mind that references should be limited to twenty-five to thirty. Authors should make use of case examples to illustrate their ideas, rather than citing exhaustive research references. You may want to recommend two or three key articles, books, or Web sites that are influential in the field, to be featured on a resource page. This can be used by readers who want to delve more deeply into a particular topic.
- All reference information should be listed as endnotes, rather than including author names in the body of the article or footnotes at the bottom of the page. The endnotes are in APA style.

Please visit http://www.pearweb.org for more information.

Gil G. Noam
Editor-in-Chief

Back Issue/Subscription Order Form

Copy or detach and send to:
Jossey-Bass, A Wiley Imprint, 989 Market Street, San Francisco, CA 94103-1741

Call or fax toll-free: Phone 888-378-2537 6:30AM – 3PM PST; Fax 888-481-2665

Back issues: Please send me the following issues at $29 each.
(Important: please include series initials and issue number, such as YD100.)

_____

_____

_____

$ _____ Total for single issues

$ _____

Shipping charges:	Surface	Domestic	Canadian
	First item	$5.00	$6.00
	Each add'l item	$3.00	$1.50

For next-day and second-day delivery rates, call the number listed above.

Subscriptions: Please __start __renew my subscription to *New Directions for Youth Development* for the year 2_____ at the following rate:

U.S.	__Individual $80	__Institutional $180
Canada	__Individual $80	__Institutional $220
All others	__Individual $104	__Institutional $254

**For more information about online subscriptions visit
www.interscience.wiley.com**

$ _____ Total single issues and subscriptions (Add appropriate sales tax for your state for single issue orders. No sales tax for U.S. subscriptions. Canadian residents, add GST for subscriptions and single issues.)

__Payment enclosed (U.S. check or money order only)
__VISA __MC __AmEx #_____ Exp. date _____

Signature _____ Day phone _____
__ Bill me (U.S. institutional orders only. Purchase order required.)

Purchase order # _____
          Federal Tax ID13559302   GST 89102 8052

Name _____

Address _____

_____

Phone _____ E-mail _____

For more information about Jossey-Bass, visit our Web site at **www.josseybass.com**

Other Titles Available

the effects of threat, stress, and traumatic events, including acts of terror, on children and youth. It addresses not only the individual repercussions of threat but also a collective approach to threat. It also illustrates important ways to prevent traumatic situations from having lifelong, negative impacts. These methods involve providing immediate intervention and fostering safety as soon as a threatening incident has occurred as well as preparing children for future threats in ways that enhance feelings of safety rather than raise anxiety.
ISBN 0-7879-7075-1

YD97 **When, Where, What, and How Youth Learn**
Karen J. Pittman, Nicole Yohalem, Joel Tolman
Acknowledging that young people learn throughout their waking hours, in a range of settings, and through a variety of means, this volume presents practical advancements, theory development, and new research in policies and infrastructures that support expanded definitions of learning. Representing the perspectives of a broad range of scholars and practitioners, chapters explore ways to connect learning experiences that happen inside and outside school buildings and during and after the school day. The contributors offer a compelling argument that communitywide commitments to learning are necessary if our nation's young people are to become problem free, fully prepared, and fully engaged.
ISBN 0-7879-6848-X

YD96 **Youth Participation: Improving Institutions and Communities**
Benjamin Kirshner, Jennifer L. O'Donoghue, Milbrey McLaughlin
Explores the growing effort in youth organizations, community development, and schools and other public institutions to foster meaningful activities that empower adolescents to participate in decision making that affects their lives and to take action on issues they care about. Pushing against long-held, culturally specific ideas about adolescence as well as institutional barriers to youth involvement, the efforts of these organizations engaged in youth participation programs deserve careful analysis and support. This volume offers an assessment of the field, as well as specific chapters that chronicle efforts to achieve youth participation across a variety of settings and dimensions.
ISBN 0-7879-6339-9

YD95 **Pathways to Positive Development Among Diverse Youth**
Richard M. Lerner, Carl S. Taylor, Alexander von Eye
Positive youth development represents an emerging emphasis in developmental thinking that is focused on the incredible potential of adolescents to maintain healthy trajectories and develop resilience, even in the face of myriad negative influences. This volume discusses the theory, research, policy, and programs that take this strength-based, positive development approach to diverse youth. It examines theoretical ideas about the nature of positive youth development, and

about the related concepts of thriving and well-being, as well as current and needed policy strategies, "best practice" in youth-serving programs, and promising community-based efforts to marshal the developmental assets of individuals and communities to enhance thriving among youth.
ISBN 0-7879-6338-0

YD94   **Youth Development and After-School Time: A Tale of Many Cities**
Gil G. Noam, Beth Miller
This issue looks at exciting citywide and cross-city initiatives in after-school time. It presents case studies of youth-related work that combines large-scale policy, developmental thinking, and innovative programming, as well as research and evaluation. Chapters discuss efforts of community-based organizations, museums, universities, schools, and clinics who are joining forces, sharing funding and other resources, and jointly creating a system of after-school care and education.
ISBN 0-7879-6337-2

YD93   **A Critical View of Youth Mentoring**
Jean E. Rhodes
Mentoring has become an almost essential aspect of youth development and is expanding beyond the traditional one-to-one, volunteer, community-based mentoring. This volume provides evidence of the benefits of enduring high-quality mentoring programs, as well as apprenticeships, advisories, and other relationship-based programs that show considerable promise. Authors examine mentoring in the workplace, teacher-student interaction, and the mentoring potential of student advising programs. They also take a critical look at the importance of youth-adult relationships and how a deeper understanding of these relationships can benefit youth mentoring. This issue raises important questions about relationship-based interventions and generates new perspectives on the role of adults in the lives of youth.
ISBN 0-7879-6294-5

YD92   **Zero Tolerance: Can Suspension and Expulsion Keep Schools Safe?**
Russell J. Skiba, Gil G. Noam
Addressing the problem of school violence and disruption requires thoughtful understanding of the complexity of the personal and systemic factors that increase the probability of violence, and designing interventions based on that understanding. This inaugural issue explores the effectiveness of zero tolerance as a tool for promoting school safety and improving student behavior and offers alternative strategies that work.
ISBN 0-7879-1441-X

NEW DIRECTIONS FOR YOUTH DEVELOPMENT
IS NOW AVAILABLE ONLINE AT WILEY INTERSCIENCE

What is Wiley InterScience?

Wiley InterScience is the dynamic online content service from John Wiley & Sons delivering the full text of over 300 leading scientific, technical, medical, and professional journals, plus major reference works, the acclaimed *Current Protocols* laboratory manuals, and even the full text of select Wiley print books online.

What are some special features of Wiley InterScience?

Wiley InterScience Alerts is a service that delivers table of contents via e-mail for any journal available on Wiley InterScience as soon as a new issue is published online.
Early View is Wiley's exclusive service presenting individual articles online as soon as they are ready, even before the release of the compiled print issue. These articles are complete, peer-reviewed, and citable.
CrossRef is the innovative multi-publisher reference linking system enabling readers to move seamlessly from a reference in a journal article to the cited publication, typically located on a different server and published by a different publisher.

How can I access Wiley InterScience?

Visit http://www.interscience.wiley.com

Guest Users can browse Wiley InterScience for unrestricted access to journal Tables of Contents and Article Abstracts, or use the powerful search engine.
Registered Users are provided with a *Personal Home Page* to store and manage customized alerts, searches, and links to favorite journals and articles. Additionally, Registered Users can view free Online Sample Issues and preview selected material from major reference works.
Licensed Customers are entitled to access full-text journal articles in PDF, with select journals also offering full-text HTML.

How do I become an Authorized User?

Authorized Users are individuals authorized by a paying Customer to have access to the journals in Wiley InterScience. For example, a university that subscribes to Wiley journals is considered to be the Customer. Faculty, staff, and students authorized by the university to have access to those journals in Wiley InterScience are Authorized Users. Users should contact their Library for information on which Wiley journals they have access to in Wiley InterScience.

ASK YOUR INSTITUTION ABOUT WILEY INTERSCIENCE TODAY!

Printed in the United States
80753LV00003B/185

9 780787 988272